HEART CLEANSE

LORI LORGEREE

WE HELP
AUTHORS

WEHELPAUTHORS.COM

Heart Cleanse

Written by Lori Lorgeree

Library of Congress Control Number: 2025914707

ISBN: 978-1-968841-02-7 *Paperback*

Published by WeHelpAuthors.com/publishing

This is a work of nonfiction. Any resemblance to actual persons, living or dead, is purely coincidental unless otherwise stated.

Cover and interior design by We Help Authors.

Printed in the United States of America

For bulk orders, please visit: **WeHelpAuthors.com/bulk**

DEDICATED TO:

Tuck

Nix

Scottie

the wisest editors

I love you!

CONTENTS

INTRODUCTION

I hope you're able to settle into a cozy place with this book and a journal. God will meet you there and draw your heart closer to His. Allow yourself to focus and dig in, spending extra time where you need, to really absorb what God is speaking to your heart and showing you in your life. I would love to hear from you with your experiences, perspectives, and questions.

Taking our thoughts captive is necessary spiritual warfare. I pray that these devotions help you do just that. Meditate on God's Word, learn more of His truths, develop a deeper relationship with Him, stay focused on Him through all of life's ups and downs, and love Him and yourself more. Examine your heart and celebrate how far you've come while pushing forward and growing more.

These devotions are designed to help you grow and identify things that need to shift in your heart. The Holy Spirit will show you areas to work on, but He will never condemn you. Be kind and compassionate to yourself as you work through things, just like you would be to a close friend if they were struggling in the same way. Just like Jesus was to everyone who came to Him.

May the waters of the Word cleanse your heart and draw you into His Presence.
Lori

Strong & Courageous

Have I not commanded you? Be strong and courageous! Do not be terrified nor dismayed, for the Lord your God is with you wherever you go.
Joshua 1:9 NASB

Have I not commanded you? Be strong and courageous. Do not be afraid; do not be discouraged, for the Lord your God will be with you wherever you go.
Joshua 1:9 NIV

Read

Joshua 1.

These definitions may be helpful as you read:

Strong - having the power to perform demanding tasks, able to withstand great force or pressure, intense, not easily damaged

Courageous - not deterred by danger or pain, brave, having the mental or moral strength to persevere and withstand danger, fear, or difficulty

Obedient - submissive to another's will, complying with orders and requests

"And after Moses, Yahweh's servant, died, Yahweh spoke to Joshua son of Nun, Moses' faithful assistant, and said, "My servant Moses is dead. Now get up! Prepare to cross the Jordan River, you and all the people. Lead them into the land that I am giving to the Israelites. Every part of the land where you march I will give you, as I promised Moses. Your borders will extend from the southern desert to the northern mountains of Lebanon, and from the great river Euphrates in the east, to the Mediterranean in the west—including all the land of the Hittites. Joshua, no one will be able to defeat you for the rest of your life! I will be with you as I was with Moses, and I will never fail nor abandon you. You must be strong and brave. You will lead the people to acquire and apportion the land that I promised their ancestors I would give them. You must remain very strong and courageous! Be faithful to obey all the teaching that my servant Moses commanded you to follow. Do not deviate from him to the right or to the left, so that you will have overwhelming success in everything you undertake. Recite this scroll of the law constantly. Contemplate it day and night and be careful to follow every word it contains; then you will enjoy incredible prosperity and success. I repeat, be strong and brave! Do not yield to fear nor be discouraged, for I am Yahweh your God, and I will be with you wherever you go!" Joshua ordered the leaders of the people: "Go through the camp and instruct the people, 'Pack your bags; for within three days you will cross the Jordan to conquer and occupy the land that Yahweh your God is giving you to possess.'" Then Joshua addressed the Reubenites, the Gadites, and the half-tribe of Manasseh: "Remember the words that Yahweh's servant Moses commanded you: 'Yahweh your God is giving you this land on the east side of the Jordan as your homeland.' Therefore, your wives, your little ones, and your livestock may remain here, but all your valiant warriors must cross over with us armed. They will take the lead and help their brothers until they take possession of the land that Yahweh your God is giving them as their homeland. Afterward, you will be free to return to your own land and possess the land that Moses, Yahweh's servant, gave you here on the east side of the Jordan." They answered Joshua: "We will do everything you have told us and will go wherever you send us. We always obeyed Moses, and we will always obey you. May Yahweh your God stand beside you as he stood with Moses. And anyone who questions your authority or disobeys whatever you command shall be put to death. So, Joshua, be strong and brave!"" Joshua 1 TPT

Think

Joshua assumes leadership of the Israelites when Moses dies - talk about big shoes to fill! But God was right there encouraging him and reassuring him that there was nothing to fear because God chose him and wasn't going to leave him. God tells him three times to be strong and courageous (verses 6, 7, & 9).

He also tells Joshua to carefully obey Him. The Israelites have seen what happens when they disobey, but (being imperfect humans just like you and me) they continue to fall into the pattern of obey and be blessed, disobey and suffer the consequences, repent and cry out to God, repeat. We'll see this throughout the book of Joshua.

When Joshua relays God's instructions to the Israelites, they respond to Joshua with, "Only be strong and courageous!" (verse 18). I love that God gave Joshua this reminder of what Moses had already spoken to all of Israel (Deuteronomy 31:6) and then specifically to Joshua in front of all of Israel (Deuteronomy 31:7) and then what God had told Joshua directly. Moses told Joshua. God told Joshua. The people told Joshua. God really wanted to make sure he had it! Confirmation from those close to us (or sometimes even a "random" stranger) can make such a huge difference.

Reflect

1. What does "strong and courageous" evoke for you? Why did God say it three times?

2. When we believe God is always with us personally, it is empowering! Do you believe down to your core that He will never leave you nor forsake you? How does that affect your perspective on situations you're facing?

3. Have you ever felt "in over your head" stepping into a new position or season in your life? How did God show up?

4. Have you ever felt like you should offer encouragement to someone but been unsure how it would be received?

Pray

God, please help us to obey You. Give us strength and courage to face challenges. Build our faith in You. Help us to see that You never leave us, that You care for us perfectly. You are in control and have the final say. Give us eternal perspective. Help us to see that You work all things for good and that sometimes the worst things we go through in this earthly life lead to the best things in our spiritual life. Help us to grow in You and honor the ways You work in us and through us.

FEARLESS

For we have heard how the Lord dried up the water of the Red Sea before you when you came out of Egypt, and what you did to the two kings of the Amorites who were beyond the Jordan, to Sihon and Og, whom you utterly destroyed. When we heard these reports, our hearts melted and no courage remained in anyone any longer because of you; for the Lord your God, He is God in heaven above and on earth below.
Joshua 2:10-11 NASB

For we have heard how the Lord dried up the water of the Red Sea for you when you came out of Egypt, and what you did to the two kings of the Amorites who were beyond the Jordan [on the east], to Sihon and Og, whom you utterly destroyed. When we heard it, our hearts melted [in despair], and a [fighting] spirit no longer remained in any man because of you; for the Lord your God, He is God in heaven above and on earth beneath.
Joshua 2:10-11 AMP

LORI LORGEREE

Read

Joshua 2.

This definition may be helpful as you read:

Fear - unpleasant emotion in anticipation of something that *may* be dangerous or harmful

"Then Joshua son of Nun secretly sent out two spies from their camp at Acacia. He told them, "Go and explore the land of Canaan, especially Jericho." They went and arrived at Jericho and entered the house of Rahab the prostitute and lodged there. The king of Jericho was told: "Some Israelites have come into the city tonight to spy out the entire land. They're in Rahab's house." So the king sent messengers to Rahab, who said to her: "Turn over the men who entered your house. They're here to spy out our land." But Rahab had already hidden the two men. "Yes," she said. "The men came to me, but I had no idea where they were from. They left at sundown, just before the city gates were closed at night. Who knows where they went. Quick! Go after them, and maybe you can catch them!" (Rahab had hidden the men on her rooftop under stalks of flax she had spread out to dry on the roof.) So the men of Jericho went out to search for the spies, and the city gates were shut behind them. They searched for them as far as where the path crosses the Jordan. Before the spies had gone to sleep, Rahab went up to the rooftop and said to them, "I know that Yahweh has given you this land. Everyone is absolutely terrified, and we are all paralyzed with fear because of you. We've heard of the miracles that accompany you and how Yahweh dried up the waters of the Red Sea for you when you left Egypt. We've heard how you utterly annihilated the two Amorite kings,

Sihon and Og, and their kingdoms who were on the other side of the Jordan. As soon as we heard it, our hearts melted with fear, and we were left with no courage among us because of you. Yahweh, your God, is the true God who rules in heaven above and on earth below. Please, solemnly swear to me by the name of Yahweh that you will show kindness to my family because I have shown kindness to you. Give me a sure sign that you will spare the lives of my father and mother, my brothers and sisters, and all their families. Don't let us be killed!" The men answered, "If you don't disclose our mission to anyone, we'll pledge our lives for yours. Then, when Yahweh gives us this land, we'll honor our promise and treat you kindly." Rahab's house was built into the city wall, so she let them down from the window by a rope. She told them, "Head for the hill country and hide. The men chasing you won't find you there. Hide for three days until they have returned, then you'll be safe to go your way." But the men warned her, "You must do what we say, or we will not be bound to the oath you made us swear. When our invasion begins, bring all your family together in your house—your father and mother, your brothers and sisters, and all their families. And tie this crimson rope in the same window through which you let us down. Remember, if anyone ventures outside your house, his death will be his own fault, not ours! But if anyone inside your house is harmed, then we will be held responsible. And if you disclose our mission, we will be released from the oath you made us swear." Rahab replied in agreement, "Let it be as you say." And she sent them away, and after they departed, she tied the crimson rope in her window. The spies went straight to the hill country and hid there for three days, until the pursuers turned back. The king's men had scoured the countryside without finding them. Then the two men came down from the hills and crossed back over the Jordan to their camp. They reported to Joshua son of Nun all that had happened to them: "Yahweh has certainly handed over the entire land into our hands! All the people of the land melt in fear before us!"" Joshua 2 TPT

Think

Rahab and her family were spared. I marvel at her being aware and bold enough to trust the spies. The Holy Spirit spoke to her and she listened and responded in faith. She risked everything.

This woman that everyone judged and looked down on was the only one in her country who had revelation of the one true living God and acted on it. This theme of God choosing the lowly is repeated so many times in the Bible - Gideon, the shepherds, the disciples, the woman at the well. This piece of the story is a good reminder to love our neighbors without judging or being prideful. We are all made in God's image, we all fall short, and we are all loved by God.

This is also a good reminder not to disqualify ourselves. Our mistakes, sins, and our past never make us unusable by God; our unwillingness is the only thing that can do that.

Reflect

1. God often uses our experiences to help us support others (see 2 Corinthians 1:3-4). Write down three things God has done for you that you could share with others to encourage them.

2. Has there been a time when you disqualified yourself even though God didn't?

3. Have you ever struggled with fear?

4. Have you had to make a decision that divided you from those closest to you?

Pray

God, please help us to spread the word of Your mighty deeds so that others can learn of You and believe. Thank You that You have done so much for us so there is so much to tell!

Please help us not to be held back by fear - fear of rejection, fear of being unqualified, fear of the unknown. Help us to be strong and courageous because we have You with us. Thank You that Your perfect love holds us. You work all things for good because You are good.

TRUST & TESTIFY

And the priests who carried the ark of the covenant of the Lord stood firm on dry ground in the middle of the Jordan while all Israel crossed on dry ground, until all the nation had finished crossing the Jordan.
Joshua 3:17 NASB

The priests who carried the ark of the covenant of the Lord stopped in the middle of the Jordan and stood on dry ground, while all Israel passed by until the whole nation had completed the crossing on dry ground.
Joshua 3:17 NIV

Read

Joshua 3.

Notice the use of LORD and Lord in verse 13.

LORD is a translation of Yahweh, God's Hebrew name.

Lord (capitalized) is a translation of Adonai, which indicates He is in control.

"Joshua was up bright and early the next morning. They broke camp, and Joshua led the Israelites from Acacia to the eastern bank of the Jordan. There they set up camp and waited until they crossed over. After three days, the leaders of the people went throughout the camp giving orders to the people, "Watch for the priests of the tribe of Levi to lift the ark of the covenant of Yahweh your God. When it starts moving, follow it so you'll know which way to go, since you've never marched this way before. Follow about a half mile behind the ark; don't go near it." Joshua instructed the people, "Get yourselves ready! Set yourselves apart for Yahweh! Tomorrow, Yahweh will perform for us great miracles!" Joshua told the priests, "Raise up the ark of the covenant and step out ahead of the people." So they lifted the ark onto their shoulders and marched in front of the people. Yahweh said to Joshua, "This very day I will begin to exalt you in the sight of all Israel so that they will realize that I am with you in the same way I was with Moses. You are to command the priests who carry the ark of the covenant with these words: 'Carry the ark to the edge of the Jordan and wade into the water.'" Joshua told the Israelites, "Come closer and listen to the words of Yahweh your God. This is how you will know for sure that the Living God is among you. As you advance into the land, he will drive out before you the Canaanites, Hittites, Hivites, Perizzites, Girgashites, Amorites, and Jebusites. Look! The ark of the covenant of the Lord of all the earth will go before you and prepare a way for you through the Jordan. Now select twelve men from among the people, one man from each tribe. The moment the feet of the priests carrying the ark of Yahweh, the Lord of all the earth, touch the water of the Jordan, a great miracle will happen! The water flowing downstream toward you will stop and pile up as if behind a dam." Now it was time for the early harvest, and the river was overflowing at flood stage. When the people broke camp to cross the Jordan, the priests went in front of them carrying the ark of the covenant on their shoulders. The very moment the priests with the ark dipped their feet in the river's edge, the water coming downstream toward them stopped flowing and piled up in a solid wall as far upstream as Adam, a place near Zarethan. Yahweh completely cut off the flow of the river so that it drained downstream toward the Desert Sea (the Dead Sea). So the people crossed over opposite Jericho. Now the priests stood firmly on dry ground in the riverbed with the ark on their shoulders. The entire nation passed by the ark as they completed their miracle-crossing on dry ground." Joshua 3 TPT

Think

The people of Jericho were already terrified because they had heard about God parting the Red Sea for the Israelites. They believed it had happened.

The Israelites in today's verses had heard from the prior generation about what God had done, but most of them had not actually been there for the crossing. I wonder if hearing those stories over the years added to their excitement that they would experience God's miraculous water-parting firsthand or if they were anxious and fearful. What if God didn't come through this time?

Also, Joshua had just told them to stay away from the ark of the covenant, but now they had to walk right past it in the middle of the river. What if they got too close? What if the water started spilling back before they safely reached the other side? It *was* flood season after all! So many things could go wrong. So many anxiety-inducing possibilities. How many situations do we face like this? Do we allow fear to paralyze us, keeping us from God's plans that bring blessings to us and others? Or do we trust God and start walking into what He's called us, letting our faith and trust grow as we go?

Reflect

1. When scary situations arise, do you run to God first or to other people?

2. Is there something you've been letting fear hold you back from doing?

3. Are there times when you tell people you "were lucky" rather than using the opportunity to give God credit?

Pray

God, please help us to walk by faith, not by sight. We can trust You because, as Joshua said, You are "the Lord of all the earth." Fill us with excitement and wonder because of all You've already done. Help us to share examples with others because when we do, it increases their faith and ours. Thank You that Your power is present in our testimonies. Make us more sensitive to Your Holy Spirit guiding us and giving us the right words to share.

REMINDER

This shall be a sign among you; when your children ask later, saying, 'What do these stones mean to you?' then you shall say to them, 'That the waters of the Jordan were cut off before the ark of the covenant of the Lord; when it crossed the Jordan, the waters of the Jordan were cut off.' So these stones shall become a memorial to the sons of Israel forever.
Joshua 4:6-7 NASB

So that this may be a sign among you; when your children ask later, 'What do these stones mean to you?' then you shall say to them that the waters of the Jordan were cut off before the ark of the covenant of the Lord; when it crossed the Jordan, the waters of the Jordan were cut off. So these stones shall become a memorial for Israel forever.
Joshua 4:6-7 AMP

Read

Joshua 4.

This definition may be helpful as you read:

Memorial - something designed to remind, preserve the memory of, or honor someone or something

"When the entire nation had finished their miracle-crossing of the Jordan, Yahweh said to Joshua, "Choose twelve men, one from each of the twelve tribes of Israel. Instruct each of them to take a stone from the riverbed, twelve stones from the very place where the priests stand with the ark. Have them carry the stones over to the place where you camp tonight." So Joshua summoned the twelve men he had selected from the Israelites, one per tribe. Joshua instructed them, "Walk out to the middle of the riverbed to the ark of Yahweh your God. Each of you choose a stone and lift it up onto your shoulder—one stone for each tribe. The stones will always be a sign to you. Someday, when your children ask you, 'Why are these stones so important?' tell them, 'The Jordan stopped flowing in front of the ark of the covenant of Yahweh—the floodwaters were completely cut off.' These stones will serve as a memorial for Israel forever." The Israelites did as Joshua commanded them. They took twelve stones according to the number of the tribes of Israel, from the middle of the riverbed, and carried them to the camp and put them there. Joshua set up the memorial stones that they had taken from the exact spot where the priests stood bearing the ark in the riverbed. They remain there to this day. While the priests remained standing in the middle of the Jordan with the ark on their shoulders, the people hurried across. All the instructions Yahweh had given to Joshua were carried out—just as Moses had told Joshua. And when Israel had finished crossing, the ark of Yahweh and the priests crossed as the people looked on. The Reubenites, the Gadites, and half the tribe of Manasseh went across, armed and ready for battle, in front of the Israelites, as Moses had commanded them. In all, about forty thousand men were equipped for battle. And they all marched before Yahweh to wage war on the plains of Jericho. On that day, Yahweh exalted Joshua before all the people. As they had stood in awe of Moses, so they stood in awe of Joshua for the rest of his life. Yahweh said to Joshua, "Command the priests carrying the ark of the covenant to come up from the Jordan." So Joshua did as he was commanded, and the priests carrying the ark of the covenant of Yahweh came up from the riverbed. And the moment their feet touched the western bank of the Jordan, the floodwaters surged back in place where they were before and returned to flood stage. The people experienced the miracle-crossing of the Jordan on the tenth day of the first month of the Jewish calendar. They established their base camp at Gilgal, east of Jericho, where Joshua set up a memorial with the twelve stones taken from the Jordan. He told the Israelites, "In time to come, when children ask their fathers, 'Why are these stones so important?' tell them, 'Here is the place where the Israelites crossed the Jordan on dry ground!' For your God, Yahweh, dried up the waters of the Jordan before your eyes until you crossed over, just as Yahweh your God did for us years ago; he dried up the Red Sea while we crossed over! He has done these miracles so that all the earth will be in awe of the mighty power of Yahweh and that you might always obey Yahweh your God!'" Joshua 4 TPT

Think

The whole nation crossed over. Wow! How long did that take? How wide was the path they walked on?

Then Joshua had to select 12 men to send back to the center to get 12 stones. Meanwhile, the Israelites stood and watched. Can you imagine what that would have been like? I envision something like the end of a race. Excitement in the air. Some people totally pumped up by the accomplishment of crossing the finish line. Others collapsing in exhaustion, having spent every last bit of their energy. Others speechless in amazement, thinking "did that really just happen???"

But in the midst of all this, stones are being gathered as reminders – tangible reminders to hold onto and pass down to future generations. Not just a reminder of a crazy thing that happened way back when. A memorial of God's goodness. His faithfulness to the people He loved. A symbol of God being capable of literally anything. Going to any lengths for His beloved children. What a God we serve!

Reflect

1. Are you going through a situation that is challenging you? Are you surrendered to God?

2. What are some reminders you have for yourself and others to be more aware of God's goodness and faithfulness?

3. God began their journey through the wilderness into the

Promised Land with parting waters to make a way for them. And He ended the journey with that display of His power and provision. Why do you think He did that? See verse 24.

4. Look for opportunities to work God's goodness into your conversations this week.

Pray

God, thank You for always being with us. You are our ever-present help in times of trouble. You are unchanging and completely reliable. Forgive us for forgetting that at times. For letting our circumstances overwhelm us and blur our vision of You and Your goodness. Please help us to establish effective reminders in our lives that point us back to You. Thank You for being our powerful Provider.

ANCHORED

For the sons of Israel walked forty years in the wilderness, until all the nation, that is, the men of war who came out of Egypt, perished because they did not listen to the voice of the Lord, to whom the Lord had sworn that He would not let them see the land which the Lord had sworn to their fathers to give us, a land flowing with milk and honey.
Joshua 5:6 NASB

For the Israelites walked forty years in the wilderness, until all the nation, that is, the men of war who came out of Egypt, died because they did not listen to the voice of the Lord; to them the Lord had sworn [an oath] that He would not let them see the land which He had promised to their fathers to give us, a land [of abundance] flowing with milk and honey.
Joshua 5:6 AMP

The Israelites had moved about in the wilderness forty years until all the men who were of military age when they left Egypt had died, since they had not obeyed the Lord. For the Lord had sworn to them that they would not see the land he had solemnly promised their ancestors to give us, a land flowing with milk and honey.

Joshua 5:6 NIV

Read

Joshua 5:1-12.

This definition may be helpful as you read:

Consequence - result or effect of an action or set of actions or conditions

"All the Amorite kings west of the Jordan and all the Canaanite kings along the coast of the Mediterranean Sea became terrified of the Israelites. For when they heard how Yahweh miraculously dried up the Jordan so that the Israelites could cross over, all their courage melted away. At that time, Yahweh commanded Joshua, "Make knives of flint and circumcise the men of Israel again." So Joshua made stone knives and circumcised all the men at a place they named Circumcision Hill. Joshua had to circumcise all the men and boys—all the fighting men. Although they had been circumcised before leaving Egypt, the male children born during the forty years they spent in the wilderness had not been circumcised. Also, by the end of that forty years, all the fighting men who had come out of Egypt had died because they had not listened to the voice of Yahweh. So Yahweh had made an oath that they would not see the land he had promised to give their ancestors, a fertile land. So he raised up their sons in their place, and Joshua circumcised them because they had not been circumcised on the way. After the circumcision was completed, the whole nation waited in the camp until their wounds had healed. Then Yahweh said to Joshua, "Today, I have rolled away your disgrace from being slaves in Egypt." For that reason, the place is named Gilgal to this day. While encamped at Gilgal, not far from Jericho, the Israelites celebrated the Feast of Passover in the evening of the fourteenth day of the month of Abib. The very next day, they ate for

the first time food grown in Canaan—roasted grain and flatbread made without yeast. On that day, when they ate the produce of the land, the manna stopped falling from heaven. The Israelites never ate manna again, but that year they enjoyed the fruit of the land of Canaan."
Joshua 5:1-12 TPT

Think

God wants us to be near Him all the time. Sometimes we run to Him when we need help, but then when the problem has passed, we start to let Him slip on the priority list. Or sometimes it's the exact opposite and when problems come, worry and fear infringe on our time with Him. It is natural for relationships to have ebbs and flows; however, it is so easy to get off course. We need to be anchored in God and guard our hearts against drifting.

The Israelites kept running to God when trouble came and then forgetting Him when life was good. They fell into serious evil and suffered some terrible consequences even though they had seen God do amazing things for them. These are the same people who walked through the Jordan. We're not talking about someone tipping a tree trunk across a cute little bubbling brook to avoid wet sandals. God pushed the river, in flood season no less, out of the way for them. They walked past impossible walls of water on both sides of them. But still they forgot and disobeyed. And that, unfortunately, is not unique to the Israelites.

We all fall short, forget, ignore the Holy Spirit's nudge, or put off doing what God wants us to do. While God always loves us and forgives us when we come back, we can experience some awful consequences for disobedient choices. Disobedience isn't limited to worshiping golden idols or committing murder. It can be as innocent-seeming as not saying something to a stranger at the grocery store when God is putting it on your heart to say it.

Reflect

1. Do you tend to run to or from God when life isn't going as planned?

2. What are some ways you can stay anchored to God and keep Him first in your life?

3. Have you ever been mad at God for letting you endure the natural consequences of your own actions? Frustrated that asking for forgiveness didn't immediately rescue you from a situation?

Pray

God, please forgive us for disobedience. Please make us aware of it and quick to correct it. Help us to take responsibility without making excuses. Thank You that You always love us and want us to draw near to You, regardless of any choices we've made or how many times we've turned away from You. Thank You that Your Word is a light on our path. Help us to guard our hearts and minds with Your truth and trust You with all that we are and all that we have.

In His Presence

He said, "No; rather I have come now as captain of the army of the Lord."
And Joshua fell on his face to the ground, and bowed down, and said to him,
"What has my Lord to say to his servant?"
Joshua 5:14 NASB

He said, "No; rather I have come now as captain of the army of the
Lord." Then Joshua fell with his face toward the earth and bowed down,
and said to him, "What does my Lord have to say to his servant?"
Joshua 5:14 AMP

"Neither," he replied, "but as commander of the army of the Lord I
have now come." Then Joshua fell facedown to the ground in reverence,
and asked him, "What message does my Lord have for his servant?"
Joshua 5:14 NIV

Read

Joshua 5:13-15.

This definition may be helpful as you read:

Holy - dedicated or consecrated to God, sacred, pure, considered worthy of spiritual respect

"When Joshua was near Jericho, he looked up and saw standing in front of him a man holding a drawn sword. Joshua approached him and said, "Are you on our side or on our enemies'?" "Neither," he replied. "I have not come to take sides but to take charge. I am the Commander of Yahweh's armies." At once, Joshua threw himself facedown to the ground and worshiped, and he said to him, "I will do whatever you command, my Lord." The Commander of Yahweh's armies said to Joshua, "Remove your sandals, for you are standing on holy ground!" And Joshua obeyed." Joshua 5:13-15 TPT

Think

I love that Joshua was fearless! Before we pick up at the end of Chapter 5, God Himself had commanded Joshua to be strong and courageous and not to be afraid or discouraged. Now God approaches him in bodily form, and Joshua is ready to attack!

Most of the time throughout the Bible, the first thing even an angel has to say is "don't be afraid." Not to Joshua. He went straight toward an unknown drawn sword. Bold and courageous!

He was standing in the Lord's presence without knowing it and then, as soon as he was told, he bowed reverentially. In many other accounts, we see people shrinking back in fear, but he bowed in honor.

Joshua asks what message the Lord has for him. How often do we come before God and tell Him how we're feeling or ask Him for what we want without asking what He wants? He cares about what we have to say, but that shouldn't be our only interaction.

Reflect

1. Has God ever shown up for you, but you've been completely oblivious?

2. Do you think of prayer as an interactive activity with God? Do you believe God desires a personal one-on-one relationship with you that you can develop?

3. The Lord told Joshua to take off his sandals. How do you observe God's Presence? What can you remove or cast aside to be closer to Him?

Pray

God, please help us to be aware of You! Help us to come to You seeking Your will. Thank You that You want a relationship with each of Your children and speak to us. All we have to do is make time to listen. Please give us peace and help us to not be distracted from You or drawn away by busyness. Thank You that You are worthy of our time, energy, and resources. When we seek You first, You take care of the other things. You provide and make a way even when we can't see one. Help us to believe.

VICTORIOUS

So the people shouted, and the priests blew the trumpets; and when the people heard the sound of the trumpet, the people shouted with a great shout, and the wall fell down flat, so that the people went up into the city, everyone straight ahead, and they took the city.
Joshua 6:20 NASB

So the people shouted [the battle cry], and the priests blew the trumpets. When the people heard the sound of the trumpet, they raised a great shout and the wall [of Jericho] fell down, so that the sons of Israel went up into the city, every man straight ahead [climbing over the rubble], and they overthrew the city.
Joshua 6:20 AMP

Read

Read Joshua 6.

"Now the gates of Jericho were bolted and barred because of the Israelites; no one could get in or out. Yahweh commanded Joshua, "See, I have given Jericho, its king and mighty warriors into your hands. March around the city with all your men of war once a day for six days. Have seven priests carry shofars in front of the ark. On the seventh day, march around the city seven times, with the priests blowing the shofars. When you hear the blare of the shofars, have all the people shout with a mighty shout of joy! Then the walls of the city will collapse before your eyes, and your whole army must charge straight in!" So Joshua son of Nun summoned the priests and instructed them: "Take up the ark of the covenant, and have seven priests carry seven shofars in front of the ark of Yahweh." And to the people he said, "Forward! March around the city and set an advance guard of armed men to march ahead of the ark of Yahweh." At Joshua's order, the seven priests carrying seven shofars advanced before Yahweh. The ark of the covenant of Yahweh followed them as they made long blasts on their shofars. The advance guard marched in front of the priests who were blowing the shofars, the rear guard marched behind the ark, and the shofars blared the whole time! Now Joshua had commanded the rest of the people, "Do not shout! Remain silent! Don't make a sound until the moment I command you to shout. Then lift up a shout with all your might!" So the ark of Yahweh circled the city once, then they all came back to the camp in Gilgal and spent the night. Joshua rose bright and early the next morning, and the priests took up the ark of Yahweh. The armed men and the seven priests carrying the seven shofars marched in front of the ark of Yahweh blowing their shofars continually, and the rear guard followed the ark of Yahweh, while the trumpets kept sounding. On the second day, they circled the city once and again returned to the camp. They repeated this pattern for six days. On the seventh day, everyone rose at daybreak, and they marched around the city in the same manner seven times. After their seventh time around, when the priests were about to blow the shofars, Joshua commanded the people: "Shout a shout of joy! Yahweh has given you the city! Jericho and everything in it are to be a devoted offering to Yahweh. But spare Rahab the prostitute and everyone in her house because she hid our spies. You must not take for yourselves anything that is dedicated to Yahweh or you will bring trouble and destruction to the entire Israelite camp! Everything made of silver, gold, bronze, and iron is sacred and devoted to Yahweh; place all of it in Yahweh's treasury!" The people were ready to shout with a great shout when they heard the shofars. As soon as they heard the blast of the shofars, they raised a massive shout of jubilee like a thunderclap, and all at once the thick walls of Jericho collapsed! Everyone rushed straight ahead and captured the city. They utterly destroyed all that was in Jericho, men and women, young and old, livestock and donkeys—everything was destroyed with the sword. Joshua told the two spies who had entered Jericho, "Go to the prostitute's house and rescue her and everyone in her house, just as you promised her." So the two spies brought out Rahab, her father, mother, brothers and sisters, and all who belonged to her, and gave them refuge outside the camp of Israel. Then they burned Jericho to the ground and all that was within it. Only the silver and gold, brass, and iron were placed into the treasury of Yahweh's house. Yet Joshua spared Rahab the prostitute, her father's family, and all that belonged to her. She lives among the Israelites to this day because she hid the two men Joshua sent to spy out Jericho. Afterward, Joshua pronounced this solemn oath: "May Yahweh curse anyone who attempts to rebuild this city, Jericho! He will pay for laying its foundation with the life of his oldest son, and for setting up its gates with his youngest son!" Yahweh's presence was with Joshua, and he became famous throughout the land." Joshua 6 TPT

Think

This passage starts with the people of Jericho having locked themselves in the city to hide behind the walls in fear. In their hiding, they could hear the trumpets and see the army encircling them, which must have just further increased their fear.

When we're going through hard times, it is important not to isolate ourselves. We need to have a trustworthy friend or two to confide in, pray with, and gain encouragement from. Sometimes God will use another person's perspective to give us the insight we need to deal with the problem, and their support can be reassuring.

God made us to be in relationship with Him and with other people. The enemy might be working hard to discourage us by making us feel less than, unqualified, incapable, or even all alone. If we are vulnerable enough to share what we're going through/thinking/feeling, a friend can encourage us and help us overcome that defeated mentality.

That being said, we need to be selective in what we share and with whom. God laid out the seven-day plan for Joshua, but he only shared one day at a time with the people. He knew what God told him, and he didn't worry about what anyone else would think or whether it sounded crazy. He just obeyed.

Armed guards in front of the ark of the covenant make me think of defending our faith. Armed guards following the ark make me think of obedience in letting the Holy Spirit lead.

Trumpets and shouts might not have seemed like the right equipment for getting through thick walls, but with God leading and the Israelites following in obedience, it was perfect.

How amazing is it that everyone was obedient? What a beautiful picture of what the Church can accomplish when walking in unity!

Oh, and the walls that came down? We're not talking about a few sheets of drywall. These walls were over 12 feet high and 6 feet thick! When we're trusting fully and expecting God to take care of us, He doesn't disappoint.

Reflect

1. Do you tend more towards isolating yourself to not let anyone see your problems or over-sharing and letting people that really shouldn't have a voice in the matter discourage you?

2. Is it possible to be "in control" and fully obedient to God simultaneously?

3. Is the Holy Spirit nudging you to do something that you've been putting off or avoiding?

Pray

God, thank You that You are victorious. You are ever-present and always make a way through every situation. Please help us to be good friends and have good friends that point back to You. Help us to remind each other that You are good and Your ways are perfect. Even when they aren't our preferred way or the easy way. We choose to be obedient to You. Thank You that You equip us for every situation. You have a plan and purpose for each of us. Sometimes You give us the big picture and other times You just give us one step at a time. Help us to trust You either way and obey.

REPENTANCE

So the Lord said to Joshua, "Stand up! Why is it that you have fallen on your face? Israel has sinned, and they have also violated My covenant which I commanded them. And they have even taken some of the things designated for destruction, and have both stolen and kept it a secret. Furthermore, they have also put them among their own things."
Joshua 7:10-11 NASB

So the Lord said to Joshua, "Get up! Why is it that you have fallen on your face? Israel has sinned; they have also transgressed My covenant which I commanded them [to keep]. They have even taken some of the things under the ban, and they have both stolen and denied [the theft]. Moreover, they have also put the stolen objects among their own things."
Joshua 7:10-11 AMP

The Lord said to Joshua, "Stand up! What are you doing down on your face? Israel has sinned; they have violated my covenant, which I commanded them to keep. They have taken some of the devoted things; they have stolen, they have lied, they have put them with their own possessions."
Joshua 7:10-11 NIV

Read

Joshua 7.

These definitions may be helpful as you read:

Sin - an immoral act, an offense against God

Disobedience - not following instructions completely

Repentance - changing your mindset and heart to turn from sin back to God

"But the Israelites violated the commandment regarding the wealth of Jericho that was to be set apart for the Lord. Achan son of Carmi, grandson of Zimri, of the clan of Zerah, from the tribe of Judah, stole some of the devoted things for himself. This ignited Yahweh's anger against Israel. Joshua sent spies from Jericho to Ai (a small city near Beth Aven, southeast of Bethel), with orders to spy out the land. So the spies left for Ai. When they returned to Joshua, they reported to him, "There is no need to trouble the whole army to conquer Ai. The people are so few that two or three thousand men could attack it and take the city." So Joshua sent three thousand troops to attack the city, but they were routed by the men of Ai. The men of Ai chased them from the city gates, down the hill as far as the quarries, cutting them down as they fled. They killed thirty-six of Joshua's men, and when Israel heard of their defeat, their hearts melted away with fear! Joshua and the elders of Israel tore their clothes and threw dust over their heads to show their sorrow. They threw themselves facedown to the ground in front of the ark of Yahweh until the evening sacrifice. Joshua cried out, "O Lord Yahweh, why did you lead these people across the

Jordan? To be defeated? To be killed by the Amorites? If only we had been content to stay on the other side of the Jordan! O Lord, what can I say now that Israel has retreated from its enemies? When the Canaanites and everyone else in the land hear about our defeat, they will gang up on us and wipe us off the face of the earth. And what then will you do about your great name?" Yahweh spoke to Joshua: "Stand up! Why are you groveling before me? Israel has sinned! They have broken the covenant which I had commanded them to keep. They have taken forbidden plunder. They have stolen from me, taken what is mine, hidden it among their belongings, and lied about it. Cursed things are among you! That is why Israel is powerless, has retreated from their enemies, and is in danger of annihilation. If you do not get rid of these cursed things from among you, I will not go with you any longer. Get up and purify the people in preparation for tomorrow. Tell them, 'This is what Yahweh, the God of Israel says: "O Israel, you have in your midst what must be devoted entirely to me! You cannot stand against your enemies until you remove the devoted things from your midst!" Tomorrow morning, you shall present yourselves by tribes. Yahweh will indicate which tribe must come forward by clans. Yahweh will indicate which clan must come forward by families. And Yahweh will indicate which family must come forward one by one. Then finally, Yahweh will expose the man caught with the devoted things, which must be destroyed by fire. Everything that man owns you must likewise destroy by fire, for he has violated the covenant of Yahweh and committed an outrageous act in Israel!'" Joshua was up at the crack of dawn and had Israel come forward by tribes, and Yahweh indicated the tribe of Judah. Joshua then had the clans of Judah come forward, and Yahweh picked out the clan of Zerah. Joshua then had the clan of Zerah come forward and Yahweh indicated the family of Zimri. Joshua then had Zimri's family come forward one by one, and Yahweh picked out Achan, the son of Carmi, son of Zimri, son of Zerah, of the tribe of Judah. Then Joshua said to Achan, "My son, give glory to Yahweh, the God of Israel, and confess. Tell me the truth and do not hide anything from him. What have you done?" "It's true," Achan said. "I've sinned against Yahweh, the God of Israel. This is what I did: I saw among the plunder an exquisite robe from Babylon, two hundred pieces of silver, and a fifty-shekel bar of gold. I wanted them badly, so I took them and buried them in my tent with the silver underneath." Joshua sent messengers who ran to the tent, and there it was! They found it buried in the middle of the tent with the silver underneath. They took the stolen objects from the tent, brought them to Joshua and all the Israelites, and displayed them in the presence of Yahweh. Then Joshua, and all Israel with him, took Achan son of Zerah along with the silver, the robe, the bar of gold, and all that belonged to him—his sons, daughters, donkeys, oxen, sheep, tent—everything. Joshua led them all to the Valley of Trouble and said, "Why have you brought all this trouble on us? Yahweh will bring trouble on you today!" Then all the people stoned Achan and his family to death. They burned up the bodies and all Achan's possessions. They raised over him a huge mound of stones that remains to this day. That is why the place was called the Valley of Trouble ever since. Afterward, Yahweh's anger subsided against Israel." Joshua 7 TPT

Think

At the beginning of this passage, we find Israel being routed by their enemies as a consequence of their disobedience. This then caused them to melt in fear (just like their enemies had been doing not so long before). Even Joshua fell into a pity party. He was scared and embarrassed and all gloom and doom. He even asks God why He brought them across the Jordan (reminiscent of his parents' generation asking why they ever left Egyptian slavery). God, in essence, tells Joshua to get up and go fix the problem.

The heartbreaking consequences are painful to read, but they really drive home the ugliness of sin and its far-reaching consequences. Sometimes we take things lightly, distinguishing between "little sins" and "big sins." But God makes no such distinction. Sin is sin and obedience is obedience. No gray area. Our society doesn't necessarily agree with that, but we need to be careful to follow God, not culture. God says there is absolute truth. There is right and wrong.

Jesus taught about our hearts and thoughts being the places where sin is measured (see Matthew 5:21-30). And in between Joshua and Jesus, Samuel taught Saul that partial obedience is not obedience at all (see 1 Samuel 15).

This chapter of Joshua ends with Achan and his family being put to death. Yet another reminder that disobedience always costs us something, but it also costs someone else something. And also an illustration of how God expects us to stand up for what is right (see Proverbs 31:8-9). When we go along with someone else's sin, we become accountable as well.

Reflect

1. Can you think of a time when you repented but still had to endure a negative consequence?

2. Have you gone against the grain and stood up for something you believe in or spoken out against an injustice? Is there something you could do right now?

3. Do you have a pattern of disobedience in a particular area of your life? It may not be something "big" but it is still so important to identify it, confess it to God, and ask Him to help you with it.

Pray

God, thank You that Your Word gives us clear instructions to live by. And Your Holy Spirit equips us to follow them. Please help us to know Your voice and obey You fully. Thank You that You are faithful to forgive when we make mistakes, sin, and disobey You. Please reveal to us anything hidden in our hearts that shouldn't be there. Help us to repent quickly and run toward You, rather than hiding or trying to "get it together" first. Help us to value truth and justice. Strengthen us to stand boldly for what is right and true according to You and Your standards. Thank You for walking with us through any negative consequences we experience and steadfastly loving us.

HIS TIMING

Behold, this day your eyes have seen that the Lord had handed you over to me today in the cave, and someone said to kill you, but I spared you; and I said, 'I will not reach out with my hand against my lord, because he is the Lord's anointed.'
1 Samuel 24:10 NASB

Behold, your eyes have seen today how the Lord had given you into my hand in the cave. Some told me to kill you, but I spared you; I said, 'I will not reach out my hand against my lord, for he is the Lord's anointed.'
1 Samuel 24:10 AMP

See, your eyes have seen how the Lord gave you to me today in the cave. Some told me to kill you, but I had pity on you. I said, 'I will not put out my hand against my leader, for he is the Lord's chosen one.'
1 Samuel 24:10 NIV

Read

1 Samuel 24.

"Now when Saul returned from pursuing the Philistines, it was reported to him, saying, "Behold, David is in the wilderness of Engedi." Then Saul took three thousand chosen men from all Israel and went to search for David and his men in front of the Rocks of the Mountain Goats. And he came to the sheepfolds on the way, where there was a cave; and Saul went in to relieve himself. Now David and his men were sitting in the inner recesses of the cave. Then David's men said to him, "Behold, this is the day of which the Lord said to you, 'Behold; I am about to hand your enemy over to you, and you shall do to him as it seems good to you.'" Then David got up and cut off the edge of Saul's robe secretly. But it came about afterward that David's conscience bothered him because he had cut off the edge of Saul's robe. So he said to his men, "Far be it from me because of the Lord that I would do this thing to my lord, the Lord's anointed, to reach out with my hand against him, since he is the Lord's anointed." And David rebuked his men with these words and did not allow them to rise up against Saul. And Saul got up, left the cave, and went on his way. Afterward, however, David got up and went out of the cave, and called after Saul, saying, "My Lord the king!" And when Saul looked behind him, David bowed with his face to the ground and prostrated himself. And David said to Saul, "Why do you listen to the words of men who say, 'Behold, David is seeking to harm you'? Behold, this day your eyes have seen that the Lord had handed you over to me today in the cave, and someone said to kill you, but I spared you; and I said, 'I will not reach out with my hand against my lord, because he is the Lord's anointed.' So, my father, look! Indeed, look at the edge of your robe in my hand! For by the fact that I cut off the edge of your robe but did not kill you, know and understand that there is no evil or rebellion in my hands, and I have not sinned against you, though you are lying in wait for my life, to take it. May the Lord judge between you and me, and may the Lord take vengeance on you for me; but my hand shall not be against you. As the proverb of the ancients says, 'Out of the wicked comes wickedness'; but my hand shall not be against you. After whom has the king of Israel gone out? Whom are you pursuing? A dead dog, a single flea? May the Lord therefore be judge and decide between you and me; and may He see and plead my cause and save me from your hand." When David had finished speaking these words to Saul, Saul said, "Is this your voice, my son David?" Then Saul raised his voice and wept. And he said to David, "You are more righteous than I; for you have dealt well with me, while I have dealt maliciously with you. You have declared today that you have done good to me, that the Lord handed me over to you and yet you did not kill me. Though if a man finds his enemy, will he let him go away unharmed? May the Lord therefore reward you with good in return for what you have done to me this day. Now, behold, I know that you will certainly be king, and that the kingdom of Israel will be established in your hand. So now swear to me by the Lord that you will not cut off my descendants after me, and that you will not eliminate my name from my father's household." And David swore an oath to Saul. Then Saul went to his home, but David and his men went up to the stronghold." 1 Samuel 24 NASB

Think

- David waited for God's timing.
- David didn't take matters into his own hands.
- David didn't seek revenge.
- David had major self-control.
- David didn't give in to peer pressure.

This passage reminds me of Proverbs 15:1 - a soft answer turns away wrath.

I'm also reminded of Abram and Sarai taking matters into their own hands to force God's promise and making a HUGE mess in the process (see Genesis 16). However, this also makes me think of how Abraham got it totally right and didn't hesitate to act when God told him to sacrifice Isaac even though it seemed to contradict God's own promise (see Genesis 22).

To all David's men, it looked like David was throwing away his chance to seize God's promise, but David wasn't swayed. Also a good reminder to be careful who we go to for counsel. When someone has hurt us, there's pretty much always someone around that will encourage "getting them back" or "giving them what they deserve." We need to avoid those voices in our lives. We can even be an example to them of godly love by responding like David.

David knew God so well, he knew this wasn't the answer to God's promise. Even though it looked so obvious to everyone around him, he knew. He had spent so much quiet time with God (and sheep!), that he knew His voice and His will.

I love that David's heart was so soft that he felt remorse just for tearing Saul's robe even though he spared Saul's life. I think the torn piece of robe had to send chills down Saul's spine, not only because of the realization that David had his life in his hands, but also because of Saul's prior encounter with Samuel.

Samuel had given Saul instructions from God about battling the Amalekites. Saul came really close to obeying all the instructions, but didn't. Samuel gave him a reminder that partial obedience is NOT obedience at all. As a consequence, God was rejecting Saul as King. Saul was upset and begging Samuel not to leave him. As Samuel walked away, Saul grabbed at him and tore off a piece of Samuel's robe. Samuel told him it symbolized Saul's kingdom being torn from him (see 1 Samuel 15). As Saul looked at David holding the torn piece of robe, that must have flashed into his mind.

Reflect

1. What are your favorite ways to hear God's voice?

2. Are you careful who else's voice you allow to guide you?

Pray

God, please help us to love others and respect that they are all made in Your image, regardless of how much we disagree with them or dislike their behavior and choices. Please help us to know You well so we can do Your will and live in wisdom and love. Help us to trust Your timing and be fully submitted to You. Thank You for Your love and guidance. Thank You that Your plans and timing are best.

FORGIVENESS

Now the Arameans had gone out in bands and had taken captive a little girl from the land of Israel; and she waited on Naaman's wife.
2 Kings 5:2 NASB

The Arameans (Syrians) had gone out in bands [as raiders] and had taken captive a little girl from the land of Israel; and she waited on Naaman's wife [as a servant].
2 Kings 5:2 AMP

Now bands of raiders from Aram had gone out and had taken captive a young girl from Israel, and she served Naaman's wife.
2 Kings 5:2 NIV

Read

2 Kings 5:1-3.

"Now Naaman, commander of the army of the king of Aram, was a great man in the view of his master, and eminent, because by him the Lord had given victory to Aram. The man was also a valiant warrior, but afflicted with leprosy. Now the Arameans had gone out in bands and had taken captive a little girl from the land of Israel; and she waited on Naaman's wife. And she said to her mistress, "If only my master were with the prophet who is in Samaria! Then he would cure him of his leprosy."
2 Kings 5:1-3 NASB

Think

This young girl was taken captive and carried away from home to become a servant in a new country. Let that sink in for a minute. How would you feel in her place? As unlike Jesus and embarrassing to admit, I may have been wishing leprosy on this guy, rather than telling him to get healed.

But this beautiful young woman wasn't harboring any bitterness. And she must have been doing good work, for them to take her seriously. If she was difficult or doing a mediocre job, they likely wouldn't have put much stock in what she said.

Her behavior is so humbling when I think of how quickly I can get frustrated or how worked up I can get about small things. May we all be quick to forgive like she did! If she had held back, Naaman wouldn't have known there was hope for him.

Reflect

1. Ask yourself "are there times I'm judging or holding a grudge when I should be encouraging and giving hope?"

2. If I'm not loving the "unlovable" am I really following God's commands?

3. With frustrating projects, never-ending deadlines, and difficult coworkers, the workplace can be such a challenging place to show God's love. Is your attitude in the right place so that others can feel God's love from you? Are you working at everything like you're doing it for God (see Colossians 3:23)?

4. Read Matthew 5:43-48 and ask God to reveal to you areas that need work and specific action steps.

Pray

God, please reveal to us anything in our hearts that needs attention. Help us to release bitterness and unforgiveness. Thank You for the beautiful example Jesus set for us. Please help us to become more like You. Give us servants' hearts that want Your will more than anything else. Thank You that all things are possible for us through the power of Your Holy Spirit!

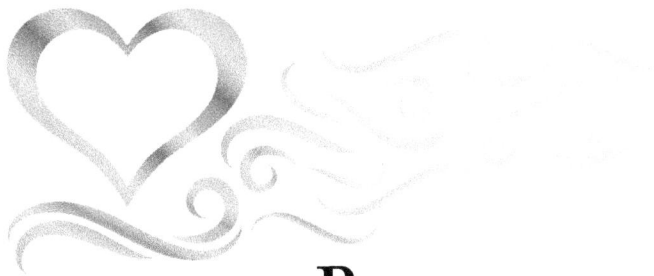

PERSPECTIVE

But Naaman was furious and went away, and he said, "Behold, I thought,
'He will certainly come out to me, and stand and call on the name of the Lord
his God, and wave his hand over the site and cure the leprosy.'"
2 Kings 5:11 NASB

But Naaman was furious and went away and said, "Indeed! I thought 'He
would at least come out to [see] me and stand and call on the name of the
Lord his God, and wave his hand over the place [of leprosy] and heal the
leper.'"
2 Kings 5:11 AMP

Read

2 Kings 5:4-14.

"And Naaman went in and told his master, saying, "The girl who is from the land of Israel spoke such and such." Then the king of Aram said, "Go now, and I will send a letter to the king of Israel." So he departed and took with him ten talents of silver, six thousand shekels of gold, and ten changes of clothes. And he brought the letter to the king of Israel, which said, "And now as this letter comes to you, behold, I have sent Naaman my servant to you, so that you may cure him of his leprosy." But when the king of Israel read the letter, he tore his clothes and said, "Am I God, to kill and to keep alive, that this man is sending word to me to cure a man of his leprosy? But consider now, and see how he is seeking a quarrel against me." Now it happened, when Elisha the man of God heard that the king of Israel had torn his clothes, that he sent word to the king, saying, "Why did you tear your clothes? Just have him come to me, and he shall learn that there is a prophet in Israel." So Naaman came with his horses and his chariots, and stood at the doorway of Elisha's house. And Elisha sent a messenger to him, saying, "Go and wash in the Jordan seven times, and your flesh will be restored to you and you will be clean." But Naaman was furious and went away, and he said, "Behold, I thought, 'He will certainly come out to me, and stand and call on the name of the Lord his God, and wave his hand over the site and cure the leprosy.' Are Abanah and Pharpar, the rivers of Damascus, not better than all the waters of Israel? Could I not wash in them and be clean?" So he turned and went away in a rage. Then his servants approached and spoke to him, saying, "My father, had the prophet told you to do some great thing, would you not have done it? How much more then, when he says to you, 'Wash, and be clean'?" So he went down and dipped himself in the Jordan seven times, in accordance with the word of the man of God; and his flesh was restored like the flesh of a little child, and he was clean." 2 Kings 5:4-14 NASB

Think

I love Elisha's message to the king - send him here because I know God will show up for him. When Naaman arrives, Elisha doesn't make a big production. He's so matter-of-fact. It's such an easy solution, he can delegate to someone else the task of relaying the instructions.

Naaman's problem seemed huge for Naaman. It was larger than life for him. But for Elisha this was just another thing his all-powerful God would fix fully and quickly! How powerful is our perspective on problems?

Naaman wanted Elisha to fix his problem but also to dwell on it with him and have a momentous occasion. That wasn't how God was working this time. Instead of being relieved that it was such a simple solution, Naaman got bent out of shape because the road to healing was short and easy, rather than twisting, turning, and treacherous. Sounds kind of ridiculous, doesn't it?

But we do that sometimes, don't we? We decide how God should work things out for us. Sometimes we tell him what we want, when we want it, and how we want it. That's not how God does His thing. He's in control and His ways are higher than ours. We need to submit to Him with faith that He will heal/fix/resolve in the perfect way at the perfect time.

Reflect

1. Do you run to God or other people first when you're facing an ugly situation?

2. Do you ask God for His perspective on your problems or do you let them loom in front of you, blocking out everything else?

3. Think of a time when God made something work out so much better than you imagined. Think of a time when unexpected blessings came from an unpleasant experience. Ask God if there's someone He wants you to share with for edification and His glory.

Pray

God, thank You so much that You are mighty and powerful and all-knowing. You see the big picture AND all the tiny details. And You care about all of it. You care about all of us. Please help us to be confident in who You are and how You work. Please help us to be open to You and Your ways. Help us to see the good in situations and their outcomes. Help us to know that sometimes You saying "no" or "not like that" is the most loving, absolute best answer for us. Thank You that You are our healer and provider and nothing is too difficult for You.

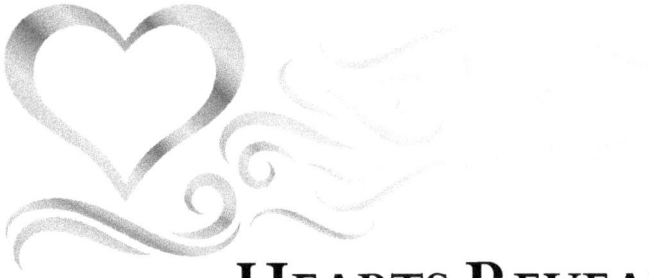

HEARTS REVEALED

But Gehazi, the servant of Elisha the man of God, thought, "Behold, my master has spared this Naaman the Aramean, by not accepting from his hand what he brought. As the Lord lives, I will run after him and take something from him."
2 Kings 5:20 NASB

Gehazi, the servant of Elisha the man of God, said to himself, "My master was too easy on Naaman, this Aramean, by not accepting from him what he brought. As surely as the Lord lives, I will run after him and get something from him."
2 Kings 5:20 NIV

Read

2 Kings 5:15-27.

"Then he returned to the man of God with all his company, and came and stood before him. And he said, "Behold now, I know that there is no God in all the earth, except in Israel; so please accept a gift from your servant now." But he said, "As surely as the Lord lives, before whom I stand, I will accept nothing." And he urged him to accept it, but he refused. Then Naaman said, "If not, please let your servant be given two mules' load of earth; for your servant will no longer offer a burnt offering nor a sacrifice to other gods, but to the Lord. Regarding this matter may the Lord forgive your servant: when my master goes into the house of Rimmon to worship there, and he leans on my hand and I bow down in the house of Rimmon, when I bow down in the house of Rimmon, may the Lord please forgive your servant in this matter." He said to him, "Go in peace." So he went some distance from him. But Gehazi, the servant of Elisha the man of God, thought, "Behold, my master has spared this Naaman the Aramean, by not accepting from his hand what he brought. As the Lord lives, I will run after him and take something from him." So Gehazi pursued Naaman. When Naaman saw someone running after him, he came down from the chariot to meet him and said, "Is everything well?" And he said, "Everything is well. My master has sent me, saying, 'Behold, just now two young men of the sons of the prophets have come to me from the hill country of Ephraim. Please give them a talent of silver and two changes of clothes.'" Naaman said, "Be sure to take two talents." And he urged him, and tied up two talents of silver in two bags with two changes of clothes, and gave them to two of his servants; and they carried them before him. When he came to the hill, he took them from their hand and deposited them in the house, and he sent the men away, and they departed. But he went in and stood before his master. And Elisha said to him, "Where have you been, Gehazi?" And he said, "Your servant went nowhere." Then he said to him, "Did my heart not go with you, when the man turned from his chariot to meet you? Is it a time to accept money and to accept clothes, olive groves, vineyards, sheep, oxen, and male and female slaves? Therefore, the leprosy of Naaman shall cling to you and to your descendants forever." So he went out from his presence afflicted with leprosy, as white as snow." 2 Kings 5:15-27 NASB

Think

A tale of two hearts is revealed in this passage - Naaman and Gehazi. Naaman has been healed and immediately believes in God and wants to serve Him fully. He wants to do everything he can to thank and honor God. He even asks for a load of dirt to take home with him because at that time gods could only be worshiped on land they were connected to. He asks forgiveness in advance for anything he may do that God wouldn't like.

What a change - how humbled and grateful he is! He wants to give Elisha anything he will accept. Elisha takes nothing to show that Naaman was given a gift by God. He won't interfere with God receiving the glory for the miraculous healing.

On the other hand, we also see Gehazi's heart revealed: a picture of greed and dishonesty. He saw an opportunity to get something for himself and seized it. Maybe that was out of character for him. Maybe it was just one moment of weakness. But he justified to himself lying to and taking from Naaman. Then he lied to Elisha to cover it up. And it cost him. His disobedience and deception cost him dearly. He paid for it with not only his health, but also the health of his descendants. What a crushing burden!

Reflect

1. What steps are you taking to live your life full of gratitude?

2. Are you serving God with everything you have without making excuses?

3. Confess taking advantage of people or circumstances. Be honest with yourself and God. Forgive the people who have taken advantage of you or deceived you.

Pray

God, thank You that You save, heal, and forgive. Please help us to recognize, confess, and turn from ways that don't honor You. Help us to be aware of Your Presence and grateful every day. May we live humbly and joyfully, putting You first and bringing You the glory You deserve.

PURPOSE, BELONGING, & LISTENING

For we are His workmanship, created in Christ Jesus for good works, which God prepared beforehand so that we would walk in them.
Ephesians 2:10 NASB

For we are His workmanship [His own master work, a work of art], created in Christ Jesus [reborn from above—spiritually transformed, renewed, ready to be used] for good works, which God prepared [for us] beforehand [taking paths which He set], so that we would walk in them [living the good life which He prearranged and made ready for us].
Ephesians 2:10 AMP

We have become his poetry, a re-created people that will fulfill the destiny he has given each of us, for we are joined to Jesus, the Anointed One. Even before we were born, God planned in advance our destiny and the good works we would do to fulfill it!
Ephesians 2:10 TPT

Read

Ephesians 2:1-10.

This definition may be helpful for you as you read:

Handiwork - something made, work done personally

"And his fullness fills you, even though you were once like corpses, dead in your sins and offenses. It wasn't that long ago that you lived in the religion, customs, and values of this world, obeying the dark ruler of the earthly realm who fills the atmosphere with his authority, and works diligently in the hearts of those who are disobedient to the truth of God. The corruption that was in us from birth was expressed through the deeds and desires of our self-life. We lived by whatever natural cravings and thoughts our minds dictated, living as rebellious children subject to God's wrath like everyone else. But God still loved us with such great love. He is so rich in compassion and mercy. Even when we were dead and doomed in our many sins, he united us into the very life of Christ and saved us by his wonderful grace! He raised us up with Christ the exalted One, and we ascended with him into the glorious perfection and authority of the heavenly realm, for we are now co-seated as one with Christ! Throughout the coming ages we will be the visible display of the infinite riches of his grace and kindness, which was showered upon us in Jesus Christ. For by grace you have been saved by faith. Nothing you did could ever earn this salvation, for it was the love gift from God that brought us to Christ! So no one will ever be able to boast, for salvation is never a reward for good works or human striving. We have become his poetry, a re-created people that will fulfill the destiny he has given each of us, for we are joined to Jesus, the Anointed One. Even before we were born, God planned in advance our destiny and the good works we would do to fulfill it!" Ephesians 2:1-10 TPT

Think

We are God's creations. We are made with a purpose. He has things planned out for us to do. We can choose to obey and do what He wants us to do (letting Him be our Lord, not just our savior) or choose to disobey and not partner with Him. The good works He has planned please Him and build His Kingdom. When we obey, others will be blessed also. We can act as conduits of God's love.

Sometimes it is difficult to know what God wants us to do in a situation. Many times we can find answers right in His Word. Even if the scriptures aren't on the same topic or don't have your name in them, God uses them to speak to You. He'll highlight different things in them that will resonate with you and show you what to do. You'll feel at peace when you know He led you to that particular passage.

God also still speaks today to us through His Holy Spirit. We need to take time to actively listen while blocking out distractions. The more we practice this, the more we will hear Him and know His will. Everything He says will line up with His written word. He won't contradict Himself, but He will speak directly to you. You can sit quietly after thanking and praising Him and ask questions. Then just wait and listen. You may hear something bubble up inside you. Don't be discouraged if it doesn't happen right away. Just keep seeking and you will find (see Jeremiah 29:13). With practice, it will become more natural and less intimidating. You'll learn the difference between your thoughts and God speaking inside you.

Reflect

1. Works can't save us (only our faith can), but they do show that we are trusting and serving God (see James 2:14-26). What are some things He's called you to do? What is a simple step you can take to get started?

2. God created you specifically and planned out important things for you in particular to do. Does that give you a sense of value and belonging? Why or why not?

3. Do you believe God wants to have a personal relationship with you that includes Him speaking to you one-on-one? Why or why not?

4. Listening is a key part of any relationship. Do you have time set aside just to listen?

Pray

God, You are so kind, loving, and creative. Thank You for intricately designing each one of us. Thank You for giving us meaning and purpose. Thank You that good works don't save us but they give us an opportunity to show our love for You and to show Your love to others. Please lead us and guide us. Help us to spend time in Your Word and listening for Your still, small voice. Thank You that You are our provider and You meet all our needs. Thank You that You faithfully provide everything we need to do everything You planned in advance for us to do. Please stretch our faith and help us to know in our innermost being that Your love never fails.

BUILDING WITH CARE

Now if any man builds on the foundation with gold, silver, precious stones, wood, hay, straw, each man's work will become evident; for the day will show it because it is to be revealed with fire, and the fire itself will test the quality of each man's work.
1 Corinthians 3:12-13 NASB

But if anyone builds on the foundation with gold, silver, precious stones, wood, hay, straw, each one's work will be clearly shown [for what it is]; for the day [of judgment] will disclose it, because it is to be revealed with fire, and the fire will test the quality and character and worth of each person's work.
1 Corinthians 3:12-13 AMP

If anyone builds on this foundation using gold, silver, costly stones, wood, hay or straw, their work will be shown for what it is, because the Day will bring it to light. It will be revealed with fire, and the fire will test the quality of each person's work.
1 Corinthians 3:12-13 NIV

The quality of materials used by anyone building on this foundation will soon be made apparent, whether it has been built with gold, silver, and costly stones, or wood, hay, and straw. Their work will soon become evident, for the Day will make it clear, because it will be revealed by blazing fire!
1 Corinthians 3:12-13 TPT

Read

1 Corinthians 3:10-15.

This definition may be helpful for you as you read:

The Day - a day of judgment, the Lord's evaluation of a believer's life for the distribution of eternal rewards

"God has given me unique gifts as a skilled master builder who lays a good foundation. Afterward another craftsman comes and builds on it. So builders beware! Let every builder do his work carefully, according to God's standards. For no one is empowered to lay an alternative foundation other than the good foundation that exists, which is Jesus Christ! The quality of materials used by anyone building on this foundation will soon be made apparent, whether it has been built with gold, silver, and costly stones, or wood, hay, and straw. Their work will soon become evident, for the Day will make it clear, because it will be revealed by blazing fire! And the fire will test and prove the workmanship of each builder. If his work stands the test of fire, he will be rewarded. If his work is consumed by the fire, he will suffer great loss. Yet he himself will barely escape destruction, like one being rescued out of a burning house." 1 Corinthians 3:10-15 TPT

Think

Our lives should be built on Christ, like a building on a foundation or a plant firmly rooted in soil. Our lives are to be lived for God's glory, building His Kingdom. Jesus paid the debt of our sin and we have our salvation and eternal life as long as we believe that, accepting the gift of what Jesus did.

However, God also has a plan and purpose for each of us that ties into His overall plan for mankind. We each have meaning and are part of something much bigger and more important than just our earthly individual lives. God has called every single one of us to lead others to Him - "Go and make disciples" (see Matthew 28:18-20). God will evaluate our lives based on the obedience of our actions. If we don't fulfill our mission, we might not lose our salvation, but we also won't be accomplishing God's plans and earning eternal rewards. And eternity is a long time to be without them!

Jesus isn't just our savior, He's our Lord. We are to obey Him and put Him in charge of our lives. Like gold that gets refined and revealed in the fire, so our hearts' posture and our efforts to serve and build the church will be revealed.

Reflect

1. What are you doing to build with care (verse 10)?

2. The precious materials Paul mentions in verse 12 are costly, while the cheap and easily-attainable materials don't endure. Are you willing to make the sacrifices and investment required to build God's Kingdom? Are there areas where you're just going through shallow motions?

3. How does thinking about the Day (verse 13) make you feel (excited, scared, etc.)? Why?

Pray

God, please help us to build something beautiful for You. Please guide us to and through the opportunities in our lives to serve You. Help us not to view any of them as small or insignificant. Give us Your perspective and confidence that when we are obeying You, nothing lacks meaning. Thank You that each of us has a role to play in Your Kingdom. Help us to view our lives and actions through an eternal lens rather than a temporal, worldly one. Thank You for including us in Your plans and making each of us valuable to You.

Precise Obedience

They had mounted the ark of God on a new cart and moved it from the house of Abinadab, which was on the hill; and Uzzah and Ahio, the sons of Abinadab, were leading the new cart.
2 Samuel 6:3 NASB

They set the ark of God on a new cart and brought it from the house of Abinadab, which was on the hill. Uzzah and Ahio, sons of Abinadab, were guiding the new cart
2 Samuel 6:3 NIV

Read

2 Samuel 6:1-8.

This definition may be helpful for you as you read:

Ark of God – also ark of the covenant, a tangible representation of God's Presence, a wooden chest covered in pure gold covered by the mercy seat

"Now David again gathered all the chosen men of Israel, thirty thousand. And David departed from Baale-judah, with all the people who were with him, to bring up from there the ark of God which is called by the Name, the very name of the Lord of armies who is enthroned above the cherubim. They had mounted the ark of God on a new cart and moved it from the house of Abinadab, which was on the hill; and Uzzah and Ahio, the sons of Abinadab, were leading the new cart. So they brought it with the ark of God from the house of Abinadab, which was on the hill; and Ahio was walking ahead of the ark. Meanwhile, David and all the house of Israel were celebrating before the Lord with all kinds of instruments made of juniper wood, and with lyres, harps, tambourines, castanets, and cymbals. But when they came to the threshing floor of Nacon, Uzzah reached out toward the ark of God and took hold of it, because the oxen nearly overturned it. And the anger of the Lord burned against Uzzah, and God struck him down there for his irreverence; and he died there by the ark of God. Then David became angry because of the Lord's outburst against Uzzah; and that place has been called Perez-uzzah to this day."
2 Samuel 6:1-8 NASB

Think

These verses have always been a tough read for me. Uzzah gets struck down dead for preventing the ark of the covenant from falling to the ground. He valued the ark and probably acted reflexively when he saw the ark falling. He had good intentions, but he was disobedient. In fact, all of them – David and his 30,000 men – were being disobedient.

The ark had been stolen by the Philistines before Saul's reign (see 1 Samuel 4-7) and then returned to Israel. David wanted to bring it back to Jerusalem. The Philistines had put the ark on a cart to return it. But the ark should not have been on a cart at all. God had given the Israelites clear instructions to use poles to carry it (see Numbers 4). David and his men were careless with something holy. They copied the Philistines' way rather than following God's instructions and it cost Uzzah his life.

God was merciful in not striking all of them down in their disobedience. God's holiness cannot be touched by our impurity, which is why Jesus had to be sacrificed to cleanse us. We need to be careful to obey God fully, seeking His will and letting Him reign over our lives, not just bless us.

Reflect

1. Does this passage make you uncomfortable? Why or why not?

2. Are there any ways you are copying the culture of the world around you, rather than lining up with God and His instructions? Ask God to reveal them to you and help you to change by the power of the Holy Spirit.

3. Do you tend to spend more time with God when things are going well and it's easy to praise Him or when things are difficult and you need help? Both are so important – He wants to be in communion with us all the time (see 1 Thessalonians 5:17).

4. 30,001 people were involved in bringing the ark back. 30,001. And somehow not a single one spoke up! We have to be able to go against the popular, easy answers when they don't honor God. Is there anything the Holy Spirit is nudging you to speak up about? It may not be a large public stand. Maybe just gently saying something to a friend (see James 5:19-20).

Pray

God, thank You for Your written Word. Please give us wisdom to understand even the uncomfortable parts. Please reveal Yourself to us and give us insight. Thank You that You are with us at all times and care for us. Please help us to value Your opinion more than anyone else's.

ENTHUSIASTIC & UNCONCERNED

And David was dancing before the Lord with all his might, and David was wearing a linen ephod. So David and all the house of Israel were bringing up the ark of the Lord with shouting and the sound of the trumpet.
2 Samuel 6:14-15 NASB

And David danced before the Lord with all his might, clad in a linen ephod [a priest's upper garment]. So David and all the house of Israel brought up the ark of the Lord with shouting and with the sound of the trumpet.
2 Samuel 6:14-15 AMP

Wearing a linen ephod, David was dancing before the LORD with all his might, while he and all Israel were bringing up the ark of the LORD with shouts and the sound of trumpets.
2 Samuel 6:14-15 NIV

Read

2 Samuel 6:9-23.

This definition may be helpful for you as you read:

Ephod - a close-fitted sleeveless vest usually worn by Hebrew priests at the altar

"So David was afraid of the Lord that day; and he said, "How can the ark of the Lord come to me?" And David was unwilling to move the ark of the Lord into the city of David with him; but David took it aside to the house of Obed-edom, the Gittite. The ark of the Lord remained in the house of Obed-edom the Gittite for three months, and the Lord blessed Obed-edom and all his household. Now it was reported to King David, saying, "The Lord has blessed the house of Obed-edom and all that belongs to him, on account of the ark of God." So David went and brought the ark of God up from the house of Obed-edom to the city of David with joy. And so it was, that when those carrying the ark of the Lord marched six paces, he sacrificed an ox and a fattened steer. And David was dancing before the Lord with all his strength, and David was wearing a linen ephod. So David and all the house of Israel were bringing up the ark of the Lord with joyful shouting and the sound of the trumpet. Then it happened, as the ark of the Lord was coming into the city of David, that Michal the daughter of Saul looked down through the window and saw King David leaping and dancing before the Lord; and she was contemptuous of him in her heart. Now they brought in the ark of the Lord and set it in its place inside the tent which David had pitched for it; and David offered burnt offerings and peace offerings before the Lord. When David had finished offering the burnt offering and the peace offerings, he blessed the people in the name of the Lord of armies. Further, he distributed to all the people, to all the multitude of Israel, both to men and women, a cake of bread, one of dates, and one of raisins to each one. Then all the people left, each to his house. But when David returned to bless his own household, Michal the daughter of Saul came out to meet David and said, "How the king of Israel dignified himself today! For he exposed himself today in the sight of his servants' female slaves, as one of the rabble shamelessly exposes himself!" But David said to Michal, "I was before the Lord, who preferred me to your father and to all his house, to appoint me as ruler over the people of the Lord, over Israel. So I will celebrate before the Lord! And I might demean myself even more than this and be lowly in my own sight, but with the female slaves of whom you have spoken, with them I am to be held in honor!" And Michal the daughter of Saul had no child to the day of her death." 2 Samuel 6:9-23 NASB

Think

David was dancing with all his might. What an enthusiastic way to celebrate what God was doing! He was leaping and dancing (verse 16). He had to have been a sweaty mess - totally unabashedly caught up in his excitement and love for God.

Just like Michal looked at David and despised him for his unusual behavior, many looked at Jesus and John the Baptizer and despised them for their non-traditional ways. John wasn't necessarily "dignified." But look how important his job was. How special he was to Jesus. How many lives he changed for the better by pointing them to Jesus. How instrumental he was in building God's Kingdom. How humble and willing to serve. We have opportunities to do all these things without even having to eat bugs in the desert (see Matthew 3:1-6).

Jesus is love. He always acted in love. He was never mean or inappropriately harsh. But He also didn't close His eyes to sin or let it slide. He called it out so that people could be released from the chains of sin and find new life in Him.

Jesus did things that were shocking and unexpected. He wasn't concerned with being prim and proper or fitting into others' expectations. He was focused on doing His Father's will and saving us - literally you and me! Many Jews were expecting a fierce warrior that would overthrow the Roman oppressors. They didn't accept Jesus because He didn't fit the bill.

Michal missed out on a happy life with King David because she couldn't let go of her preconceived notions of how he should and should not behave. I don't want to miss God's best for me by spurning anything that doesn't look the way I think it should or come in the time I want it.

Reflect

1. Michal was jealous. She didn't want all the girls seeing her husband without all his kingly layers on. Jealousy either indicates there's a problem in the relationship that needs to be addressed or a wound from a different relationship that needs to be identified and resolved. Maybe not even with the other person but in a way

that allows you to heal. Have you had a time where jealousy caused a relationship problem for you?

2. Human nature is to worry about what others think. However, God works everything for the good of those who love Him - you and me (Romans 8:28)! If He prompts you to do something unexpected, will you obey?

Pray

God, please help us to guard our hearts and stay pure. Please help us to recognize when we are jealous or judgmental so that we can repent. Humble us to value others and live for You. Thank You that we can be of service to You. May we be caught up in our love for You to the point that we are unconcerned with what others think.

REST

All things have been handed over to Me by My Father; and no one knows the Son except the Father; nor does anyone know the Father except the Son, and anyone to whom the Son wills to reveal Him.
Matthew 11:27 NASB

All things have been handed over to Me by My Father; and no one fully knows and accurately understands the Son except the Father; and no one fully knows and accurately understands the Father except the Son, and anyone to whom the Son [deliberately] wills to reveal Him.
Matthew 11:27 AMP

You have entrusted me with all that you are and all that you have. No one fully and intimately knows the Son except the Father. And no one fully and intimately knows the Father except the Son. But the Son is able to unveil the Father to anyone he chooses.
Matthew 11:27 TPT

Read

Matthew 11:27-30.

These definitions may be helpful for you as you read:

Gentle - kind and quiet nature, tender, meek, soothing

Humble - unpretentious, modest, fully submitted to God

"All things have been handed over to Me by My Father; and no one knows the Son except the Father; nor does anyone know the Father except the Son, and anyone to whom the Son determines to reveal Him. Come to Me, all who are weary and burdened, and I will give you rest. Take My yoke upon you and learn from Me, for I am gentle and humble in heart, and you will find rest for your souls. For My yoke is comfortable, and My burden is light." Matthew 11:27-30 NASB

Think

Many of us are familiar with Matthew 11:28 because we are desperate for rest in our hectic, jam-packed lives. But I think we often skip past the verses leading up to this beautiful statement Jesus made. We can't really understand who Jesus is and what He's offering without revelation from the Father. Perhaps making space for Jesus to enlighten us and develop our relationship with Him is where we truly find rest.

What makes us weary and burdened? Jesus tells us in John 15 that we can't do anything without Him. Striving, not relying on God, pride, legalism -

these wear us out and put heavy burdens on us that we weren't meant to have.

What does God's rest mean? Peace, rejuvenation, renewal, security. When we trust God and accept the free gifts He's given us, we will find a new rhythm in our lives. He loves us and we can't earn salvation or be "good enough" on our own. We don't "work hard enough" to win God's grace. He gives it and we just say, "yes, please!" Trust that His plans are good for You and His timing is right.

What does it mean to take His yoke? Submit to Him. Partner with Him. Fall into step with Him. Learn His ways. Stop struggling and running. Accept Him as Lord in addition to Savior.

We defined gentle and humble above, but looking at what they aren't is also helpful.

Gentle means:
- Not violent
- Not harsh
- Not loud
- Not overwhelming
- Not severe
- Not hard
- Not forceful

Humble means:
- Not proud
- Not arrogant
- Not haughty
- Not self-reliant

Jesus is waiting for us with no condemnation, no guilt, and open arms. He's inviting us to leave everything behind and focus on Him. When we breathe deeply of His love and grace, how can our fears and worries not start to dissolve? When we have a true revelation of Him, how can our focus not shift?

Reflect

1. We can't know the Father without revelation from Jesus. Spend some quiet time seeking a fresh revelation from God.

2. Are you submitted to God? What is an area you can commit to surrendering fully to Him?

3. How does taking His yoke upon you make you feel? Why?

Pray

God, thank You for loving us and meeting us where we are. Please help us to surrender to You and delight in our time with You. Give us true rest that only You can provide. Thank You for helping us to put down the burdens we shouldn't be carrying and assisting us with Your yoke.

Holy

Therefore, prepare your minds for action, keep sober in spirit, set your hope completely on the grace to be brought to you at the revelation of Jesus Christ.
1 Peter 1:13 NASB

So prepare your minds for action, be completely sober [in spirit—steadfast, self-disciplined, spiritually and morally alert], fix your hope completely on the grace [of God] that is coming to you when Jesus Christ is revealed.
1 Peter 1:13 AMP

So then, prepare your hearts and minds for action! Stay alert and fix your hope firmly on the marvelous grace that is coming to you. For when Jesus Christ is unveiled, a greater measure of grace will be released to you.
1 Peter 1:13 TPT

Read

1 Peter 1:13-21.

"So then, prepare your hearts and minds for action! Stay alert and fix your hope firmly on the marvelous grace that is coming to you. For when Jesus Christ is unveiled, a greater measure of grace will be released to you. As God's obedient children, never again shape your lives by the desires that you followed when you didn't know better. Instead, shape your lives to become like the Holy One who called you. For Scripture says: "You are to be holy, because I am holy." Since you call on him as your heavenly Father, the impartial Judge who judges according to each one's works, live each day with holy awe and reverence throughout your time on earth. For you know that your lives were ransomed once and for all from the empty and futile way of life handed down from generation to generation. It was not a ransom payment of silver and gold, which eventually perishes, but the precious blood of Christ—who like a spotless, unblemished lamb was sacrificed for us. This was part of God's plan, for he was chosen and destined for this before the foundation of the earth was laid, but he has been made manifest in these last days for you. It is through him that you now believe in God, who raised him from the dead and glorified him, so that you would fasten your faith and hope in God alone."
1 Peter 1:13-21 TPT

Think

Belief requires action. We become double-minded when our head and heart aren't in agreement. We need alignment to move forward in belief. We must have our eyes, heart, and hope fixed on Jesus and His grace.

Jesus has already been revealed to us to some extent to even receive new birth. As we press in, more and more is revealed. Verse 13 isn't about waiting for a second coming. It's about seeking to know Him more *now* and understand Him more *now*!

Be intentional to become more like Him. He made us in His image. He called us. He chose us. He wants us to be like Him. We become like Him when we spend time with Him.

Live with holy awe and reverence for Him. He sees all and knows all. We can't fake Him out. Be sincere.

We're not stuck in our sin or useless tradition. Jesus rescued us with His own perfect life! God's plan from the very beginning was to love, choose, and rescue us!

Reflect

1. Are you spending time listening for God to speak to your heart?

2. What's an area of your life He's calling you to transform?

3. Do your mind and your heart both fully believe that God chose you specifically to know Him personally? Why or why not?

Pray

God, please bring our hearts and minds into alignment. Reveal to us any areas where we believe with one and not the other. Thank You for these clear instructions to live by. Thank You for sacrificing Jesus to give us a brand new life in You. Help us to be watchful so that we can obediently partner with You. The only reason for us to be hopeful is You. Help us to express our hope, faith, and love by the way we live. Let the words of our mouths and the thoughts of our hearts be pure and pleasing to You. Cleanse us and guide us.

Behind the Scenes

and he goes to bed at night and gets up daily, and the seed sprouts and grows—how, he himself does not know.
Mark 4:27 NASB

and he goes to bed at night and gets up every day, and [in the meantime] the seed sprouts and grows; how [it does this], he does not know.
Mark 4:27 AMP

Night and day, whether he sleeps or gets up, the seed sprouts and grows, though he does not know how.
Mark 4:27 NIV

He goes to bed and gets up, day after day, and the seed sprouts and grows tall, though he knows not how.
Mark 4:27 TPT

Read

Mark 4:26-29.

"Jesus also told them this parable: "God's kingdom realm is like someone spreading seed on the ground. He goes to bed and gets up, day after day, and the seed sprouts and grows tall, though he knows not how. All by itself it sprouts, and the soil produces a crop; first the green stem, then the head on the stalk, and then the fully developed grain in the head. Then, when the grain is ripe, he immediately puts the sickle to the grain, because harvest time has come." Mark 4:26-29 TPT

Think

This passage is just four short verses and, sadly, is easy to gloss over/speed through. But it contains so much wisdom for us. Jesus is telling us more about what God's Kingdom is like. God is the King. He is in control. In verse 27, God makes the seed grow. He works things out even when we can't see what He's doing.

Seeds growing also teach us about cause and effect, sowing and reaping. When the seed is planted, something is set in motion. There will be a result. What we put into our hearts and minds will come out. What comes out of our mouths is generally reflective of what is in our hearts. Proverbs 4:23 warns us, "Above all else, guard your heart, for everything you do flows from it."

Taking that further, our words and actions scatter seeds to others. What we're saying and doing is going into other people's hearts and minds. Our lives need to be pure, encouraging, and life-giving. We need to be sharing God's love and scattering more of His seed. Just like a mature plant gives off more seeds of its own kind.

Maturing in Christ also requires us to trust His timing. The plant grows according to its designed schedule. The man doesn't put the sickle to it until it is ripe (ready). Sometimes I struggle with being impatient and trying to get ahead of myself or procrastinating doing what I know I'm supposed to do. But God's timing is ALWAYS better than mine. I have to trust that and act accordingly.

Reflect

1. Do you struggle to trust God's timing (in general or maybe in a particular area)?

2. Are you actively guarding your heart? Is there something you need God to help you remove?

3. Are your words life-giving and scattering the right seeds?

Pray

God, thank You so much for the treasure of Your Word. Please help us to cherish it and give You time and space to reveal Your wisdom through it. Please forgive us for the times when we've used our words in dishonoring ways or haven't said the words You've intended for us to say. Help us to share Your love and Good News with others. And help us to trust Your perfect timing. Thank You for faithfully providing and working on our behalf.

CALMING THE STORM

He said to them, "Why are you afraid, you men of little faith?" Then He got up and rebuked the winds and the sea, and it became perfectly calm.
Matthew 8:26 NASB

But Jesus reprimanded them. "Why are you gripped with fear? Where is your faith?" Then he stood and rebuked the storm, saying, "Be still!" And instantly it became perfectly calm.
Matthew 8:26 TPT

And He got up and rebuked the wind and said to the sea, "Hush, be still." And the wind died down and it became perfectly calm.
Mark 4:39 NASB

He got up, rebuked the wind and said to the waves, "Quiet! Be still!" Then the wind died down and it was completely calm.
Mark 4:39 NIV

So they shook him awake, saying, "Teacher, don't you even care that we are all about to die!" Fully awake, he rebuked the storm and shouted to the sea, "Hush! Be still!" All at once the wind stopped howling and the water became perfectly calm.
Mark 4:39 TPT

And He said to them, "Where is your faith?" But they were fearful and amazed, saying to one another, "Who then is this, that He commands even the winds and the water, and they obey Him?"
Luke 8:25 NASB

Then Jesus said to them, "Why are you fearful? Have you lost your faith in me?" Shocked, they said with amazement to one another, "Who is this man who has authority over winds and waves that they obey him?"
Luke 8:25 TPT

Read

Matthew 8:23-27, Mark 4:35-41, and Luke 8:22-25. These three authors capture the same event through each of their own perspectives.

"They all got into a boat and began to cross over to the other side of the lake. And Jesus, exhausted, fell asleep. Suddenly a violent storm developed, with waves so high the boat was about to be swamped. Yet Jesus continued to sleep soundly. The disciples woke him up, saying, "Save us, Lord! We're going to die!" But Jesus reprimanded them. "Why are you gripped with fear? Where is your faith?" Then he stood and rebuked the storm, saying, "Be still!" And instantly it became perfectly calm. The disciples were astonished by this miracle and said to one another, "Who is this Man? Even the wind and waves obey his Word."" Matthew 8:23-27 TPT

"That same day, after it grew dark, Jesus said to his disciples, "Let's cross over to the other side of the lake." Leaving the crowd behind, the disciples got into the boat in which Jesus was already sitting, and they took him with them. Other boats sailed with them. Suddenly, as they were crossing the lake, a ferocious storm arose, with violent winds and waves that were crashing into the boat until it was nearly swamped. But Jesus was calmly sleeping in the stern, resting on a cushion. So they shook him awake, saying, "Teacher, don't you even care that we are all about to die!" Fully awake, he rebuked the storm and shouted to the sea, "Hush! Be still!" All at once the wind stopped howling and the water became perfectly calm. Then he turned to his disciples and said to them, "Why are you so afraid? Haven't you learned to trust yet?" But they were overwhelmed with fear and awe and said to one another, "Who is this man who has such authority that even the wind and waves obey him?"" Mark 4:35-41 TPT

"One day Jesus said to his disciples, "Let's get in a boat and go across to the other side of the lake." So they set sail, and soon Jesus fell asleep. But a fierce wind arose and became a violent squall that threatened to swamp their boat. Alarmed, the disciples woke Jesus up and said, "Master, Master, we're sinking! Don't you care that we're going to drown?" With great authority Jesus rebuked the howling wind and surging waves, and instantly they became calm. Then Jesus said to them, "Why are you fearful? Have you lost your faith in me?" Shocked, they said with amazement to one another, "Who is this man who has authority over winds and waves that they obey him?"" Luke 8:22-25 TPT

Think

These men had spent a lot of time in these waters that were known for frequent, sudden storms. They'd been through plenty of them. How horrendous did this one have to be for them to be terrified and unsure if they would even be able to survive?

When they brought their fear to Jesus, He immediately took care of things for them. He exceeded their expectations and amazed them. Even though they went to Him looking for His help, they were still shocked when they received it. This encounter revealed something more to them. When we let Jesus get us through the storm, we grow closer to Him and learn more about Him with our hearts, not just our minds. Storms can be a conduit of incredible spiritual blessings if we surrender to God in them. Sometimes we need hands-on training, real life experience to mature in an area.

I also love that this passage shows Jesus as fully human. He was tired after ministering. He wanted to head across to the quieter side of the lake to get a break. He reclines in the gentle rocking of the boat and falls into a deep sleep.

Reflect

1. What is a storm you're facing right now?

2. Can you think of a difficult experience that resulted in you growing closer to God and/or learning something more about Him?

3. Are you able to sleep soundly on a regular basis? If not, why?

Pray

God, thank You for being with us in all the storms of life. Thank You for giving us opportunities to draw closer to You and know You more fully. Reveal Yourself to us in new ways. Help us to find peace and rest in You. We have nothing to fear when we're aware of Your Presence.

PROGRESS

But immediately Jesus spoke to them, saying, "Take courage, it is I; do not be afraid."
Matthew 14:27 NASB

Then Jesus said, "Be brave and don't be afraid. I am here!"
Matthew 14:27 TPT

Seeing them straining at the oars—for the wind was against them—at about the fourth watch of the night, He came to them, walking on the sea; and He intended to pass by them.
Mark 6:48 NASB

He saw the disciples straining at the oars, because the wind was against them. Shortly before dawn he went out to them, walking on the lake. He was about to pass by them,
Mark 6:48 NIV

The wind was against the disciples and he could see that they were straining at the oars, trying to make headway. When it was almost morning, Jesus came to them, walking on the surface of the water, and he started to pass by them.
Mark 6:48 TPT

So they were willing to take Him into the boat, and immediately the boat was at the land to which they were going.
John 6:21 NASB

Then they were willing to take him into the boat, and immediately the boat reached the shore where they were heading.
John 6:21 NIV

Read

Matthew 14:22-33, Mark 6:45-52, and John 6:16-21. These three authors capture the same event through each of their own perspectives.

"As soon as the people were fed, Jesus told his disciples to get into their boat and to go to the other side of the lake while he stayed behind to dismiss the people. After the crowds dispersed, Jesus went up into the hills to pray. And as night fell he was there praying alone. But the disciples, who were now in the middle of the lake, ran into trouble, for their boat was tossed about by the high winds and heavy seas. At about four o'clock in the morning, Jesus came to them, walking on the waves! When the disciples saw him walking on top of the water, they were terrified and screamed, "A ghost!" Then Jesus said, "Be brave and don't be afraid. I am here!" Peter shouted out, "Lord, if it's really you, then have me join you on the water!" "Come and join me," Jesus replied. So Peter stepped out onto the water and began to walk toward Jesus. But when he realized how high the waves were, he became frightened and started to sink. "Save me, Lord!" he cried out. Jesus immediately stretched out his hand and lifted him up and said, "What little faith you have! Why would you let doubt win?" And the very moment they both stepped into the boat, the raging wind ceased. Then all the disciples bowed down before him and worshiped Jesus. They said in adoration, "You are truly the Son of God!"" Matthew 14:22-33 TPT

"After everyone had their meal, Jesus instructed his disciples to get back into the boat and go on ahead of him and sail to the other side to Bethsaida. So he dispersed the crowd, said good-bye to his disciples, then slipped away to pray on the mountain. As night fell, the boat was in the middle of the lake and Jesus was alone on land. The wind was against the disciples and he could see that they were straining at the oars, trying to make headway. When it was almost morning, Jesus came to them, walking on the surface of the water, and he started to pass by them. When they all saw him walking on the waves, they thought he was a ghost and screamed out in terror. But he said to them at once, "Don't yield to fear. Have courage. It's really me—I Am!" Then he came closer and climbed into the boat with them, and immediately the stormy wind became still. They were completely and utterly overwhelmed with astonishment. Their doubting hearts had not grasped his authority and power over all things in spite of just having witnessed the miraculous feeding." Mark 6:45-52 TPT

"After waiting until evening for Jesus to return, the disciples went down to the lake. But as darkness fell, he still hadn't returned, so the disciples got into a boat and headed across the lake to Capernaum. By now a strong wind began to blow and was stirring up the waters. The disciples had rowed about halfway across the lake when all of a sudden they caught sight of Jesus walking on top of the waves, coming toward them. The disciples panicked, but Jesus called out to them, "Don't be afraid. You know who I am." They were relieved to take him in, and the moment Jesus stepped into the boat, they were instantly transported to the other side!" John 6:16-21 TPT

Think

These verses recount the second storm the disciples are caught in. Jesus had showed them He would protect them when He was with them the first time. Now, He sent them out without Him. Jesus was helping them grow their faith step by step. He was tenderly nudging them along. He knew before long they would need to be able to have faith without seeing Him physically with them.

The disciples were being obedient. Jesus told them to get into the boat without Him and go across to the other side. But He didn't make it easy for them. A storm came, winds were fighting against them, and they seemed to be making no progress even though they were following instructions. How often does this happen to us?

We get so frustrated because we're trying to obey God, but it doesn't appear to be going right. We aren't seeing the results we expect and we feel all kinds of feels that aren't exactly love and faith. But we are told to live by faith, not by sight (see Hebrews 11:1 and 2 Corinthians 5:7). Maybe the results are exactly what God has in mind - increased faith, communion with Him, drawing closer to Him.

Mark says Jesus wasn't even coming out to get into the boat with them. He was just going to walk right past. This may seem harsh at first glance, but we have to remember Jesus is literally love in the flesh. How could that be an act of love? He was giving them an opportunity to grow their faith. He could see they were having trouble and came to reassure them. Seeing He was out there might have been enough of a reminder that they were doing what He instructed and He had brought them through plenty of other troubles.

But this time, Jesus showing up scared them instead of comforting them. When we start expecting God to do things a certain way, we can lose sight of Him and shift into an unhealthy perspective. We can miss what He's doing and why He's doing it just like the disciples in this situation.

When the disciples stopped being afraid and brought Him into the boat with them, IMMEDIATELY they reached their destination. The struggle ended as soon as their focus was back on Him. Fear and frustration were instantly gone. Miraculously, they skipped the last couple of miles rowing. Jesus hadn't been trying to strengthen their bodies and help them gain rowing stamina. He was teaching them to trust Him no matter what His instructions were and what their own view of their progress was. This was another step in the right direction, and He would continue to patiently help them.

Even His comment about having little faith was said in love. He wasn't accusing or deriding. His comment shows that His intent was to increase their faith. It hadn't quite reached the level they would need, but they were progressing.

Reflect

1. Have you heard the saying "progress over perfection?" Do you think it applies to this story? Is it something you need to remind yourself occasionally to keep moving forward rather than dwelling on mistakes?

2. Have you experienced frustration and/or fear at times when your circumstances aren't lining up with your expectations? Think of a painful experience you've already come through that you can

look back and see clearly what God was doing. Now can you think of a current situation that you might need to look at from a new perspective?

3. Do you find it difficult to believe everything Jesus said and did was in love? Why or why not?

Pray

God, please help us to see You clearly in all situations. Open our eyes to Your goodness and faithfulness. Continue to grow our faith and trust in You. Thank You that You never leave us and You always bring beauty out of ashes. You give us Your love and power, not fear. Help us to recognize when fear and frustration are overtaking us and reject those thoughts. Remind us of who You are and our place in Your family.

PERSISTENCE

now, will God not bring about justice for His elect who cry out to Him day and night, and will He delay long for them?
Luke 18:7 NASB

And will not [our just] God defend and avenge His elect [His chosen ones] who cry out to Him day and night? Will He delay [in providing justice] on their behalf?
Luke 18:7 AMP

Don't you know that God, the true judge, will grant justice to all his chosen ones who cry out to him night and day? He will pour out his Spirit upon them. He will not delay to answer you and give you what you ask for.
Luke 18:7 TPT

Read

Luke 18:1-8.

"Now He was telling them a parable to show that at all times they ought to pray and not become discouraged, saying, "In a certain city there was a judge who did not fear God and did not respect any person. Now there was a widow in that city, and she kept coming to him, saying, 'Give me justice against my opponent.' For a while he was unwilling; but later he said to himself, 'Even though I do not fear God nor respect any person, yet because this widow is bothering me, I will give her justice; otherwise by continually coming she will wear me out.'" And the Lord said, "Listen to what the unrighteous judge said; now, will God not bring about justice for His elect who cry out to Him day and night, and will He delay long for them? I tell you that He will bring about justice for them quickly. However, when the Son of Man comes, will He find faith on the earth?"" Luke 18:1-8 NASB

Think

Always pray. Never give up. Persist in faith. This brief parable is full of hope. Even when people aren't concerned with doing right, God can work them into His plans and use them for our good.

The judge in this parable is NOT God. God cares. God answers prayers in a timely manner (although not always in our preferred timing). He doesn't put us off. His is just and faithful. We need to pray with faith. We need to bring God into the details of our lives; pray without ceasing (see 1 Thessalonians 5:17).

Sometimes it becomes more difficult to pray with faith as time goes by and we aren't seeing results. Those situations force us to really cling to God in faith, to live by faith not by sight (see 2 Corinthians 5:7).

Reflect

1. What does it mean to "always pray?"

2. What does it mean to live by faith (see Hebrews 11:1)?

3. Is there something you need to recommit to seeking God persistently for or about?

4. Do you ever feel like God is like the unjust judge? Like you have to keep hounding Him and can't understand why He doesn't seem to care or respond? Spend a few minutes remembering that He's a good Father that loves right and hates evil.

Pray

God, thank You for loving us. Your very nature is love. You require no persuading when it comes to wanting the best for us. Please give us clarity that You're always working for our good. Thank You that we have the privilege of being in constant communication with You throughout our days. Please increase our faith and encourage us when we are waiting for results.

SURRENDER

For I am the Lord your God who takes hold of your right hand, Who says to you, 'Do not fear, I will help you.'
Isaiah 41:13 NASB

I am Yahweh, your mighty God! I grip your right hand and won't let you go! I whisper to you: 'Don't be afraid; I am here to help you!'
Isaiah 41:13 TPT

No longer do I call you slaves, for the slave does not know what his master is doing; but I have called you friends, because all things that I have heard from My Father I have made known to you.
John 15:15 NASB

I have never called you 'servants,' because a master doesn't confide in his servants, and servants don't always understand what the master is doing. But I call you my most intimate and cherished friends, for I reveal to you everything that I've heard from my Father.
John 15:15 TPT

Read

Isaiah 41:9-13 and John 15:14-15.

These definitions may be helpful for you as you read:

Dismayed - having lost courage or resolution, distressed or anxious

Disgraced - no longer respected, fallen from a position of power or favor, made ashamed

"I drew you to myself from the ends of the earth and called you from its farthest corner. I say to you: 'You are my servant; I have chosen you. I have not rejected you! Do not yield to fear, for I am always near. Never turn your gaze from me, for I am your faithful God. I will infuse you with my strength and help you in every situation. I will hold you firmly with my victorious right hand.' "All who rage against you will be ashamed and disgraced. All who contend with you will perish and disappear. You will look for your enemies in vain; those who war against you will vanish without a trace! I am Yahweh, your mighty God! I grip your right hand and won't let you go! I whisper to you: 'Don't be afraid; I am here to help you!'"
Isaiah 41:9-13 TPT

"You show that you are my intimate friends when you obey all that I command you. I have never called you 'servants,' because a master doesn't confide in his servants, and servants don't always understand what the master is doing. But I call you my most intimate and cherished friends, for I reveal to you everything that I've heard from my Father."
John 15:14-15 TPT

Think

These verses in Isaiah are full of passion and encouragement:

- God is with us.

- God is our God.

- Don't fear.

- Don't be dismayed.

- God strengthens, helps, and upholds us.

- Our enemies will be ashamed, disgraced, brought out of existence.

And my very favorite part (v. 13): **He holds our hand!** Just think of God Himself holding your hand telling you not to be afraid because He will help you. Wow!

If we truly believe God strengthens, helps, and upholds, why would we ever be afraid or dismayed? If something else is causing us to feel that way, we need to present it to God and surrender it (see Philippians 4:6-7). This may take some wrestling and more than one time. In that surrender, we gain God's perspective and are reminded that the spiritual things are what last forever, not the earthly things. Whatever is stressing you out is nothing compared to our powerful, beautiful God. With God holding our hand, doesn't anything seem possible?

John 15, tells us that we are Jesus's friends when we obey Him. Servants don't know their master's business, but friends do. Because of Jesus, we get to know the Father. We are still to serve Him, but our relationship goes beyond servant and master. The Holy Spirit reveals God's plans to us so that we can obey and participate in making God's will be done on earth.

Reflect

1. Read Galatians 4:1-7. An underaged heir is like a servant, just as we are servants of sin until we know Jesus. According to these verses how do we transition from servant to heirs? How does this change your daily life?

2. What has you feeling dismayed or disgraced today? Can you identify when it first became an issue for you and/or what brought it into your life?

3. Are you comfortable with the thought of God holding your hand and being your friend? Why or why not?

Pray

God, thank You that we are never alone. Please give us Your perspective. Show us what true surrender and strong faith look like. Thank You for Your love and friendship. Thank You, Holy Spirit, for fresh revelation and help being obedient.

Unwavering

If it be so, our God whom we serve is able to rescue us from the furnace of blazing fire; and He will rescue us from your hand, O king. But even if He does not, let it be known to you, O king, that we are not going to serve your gods nor worship the golden statue that you have set up.

Daniel 3:17-18 NASB

If the God we serve truly exists, then he will save us from death at your hand, O king. So, if you throw us into the fiery furnace, our God is able to save us. But even if he does not save us, you can be sure, O king, that we would not serve your gods or worship the golden statue you have erected.

Daniel 3:17-18 TPT

Read

Daniel 3.

"King Nebuchadnezzar had a golden statue made that was sixty cubits high and six cubits wide. He erected the statue on the plain of Dura in the province of Babylon. He then ordered an assembly of his princes, magistrates, and governors, as well as the counselors, treasurers, judges, sheriffs, and all the other provincial authorities, that they should be present at the dedication of the statue he had erected. So all these officials gathered in front of the golden statue that the king had made. Then a herald made the loud proclamation: "Attention everyone! Listen to what the king commands of you—you of every nation and language. When you hear the ram's horn, and the music of the flute, the lyre, the ten-stringed harp, the triangular harp, the drums, and all the other instruments, you will bow down to the ground and worship the golden statue that King Nebuchadnezzar has made. Whoever does not bow down to worship it will immediately be thrown into a white-hot fiery furnace." Therefore, at the set time, as soon as they heard the musical instruments, those present from all nations and languages bowed down and worshiped the golden image that King Nebuchadnezzar had set up. At that point, certain Babylonian astrologers approached the king and maliciously denounced the Jews. They said to King Nebuchadnezzar: "O king, live forever! You issued a royal decree, O king, that when everyone hears the ram's horn and the music begins they must bow down to the ground and worship the golden image. And whoever does not bow down and worship it will be thrown inside a white-hot fiery furnace. Yet, the prominent Jews, whom you have appointed administrators of the province of Babylon, have greatly disrespected you, Your Majesty. Their names are Shadrach, Meshach, and Abednego. They do not serve your gods nor worship the golden image you have set up." Upon hearing this, King Nebuchadnezzar flew into a furious rage and ordered Shadrach, Meshach, and Abednego to be brought before him. When these men came before the king, he asked them, "Is it true, Shadrach, Meshach, and Abednego, that you do not serve my gods or worship the golden statue that I erected? I now give you one more chance. When you hear the ram's horn and the music of the flute, the lyre, the ten-stringed harp, the triangular harp, the drums, and all the other instruments, you will bow down to the ground and worship the golden statue I have made. But if you refuse to worship it, you will be thrown immediately into a white-hot fiery furnace. So now, who is the god that can save you from my power?" Shadrach, Meshach, and Abednego answered King Nebuchadnezzar: "We have no need to offer you a defense in this matter. If the God we serve truly exists, then he will save us from death at your hand, O king. So, if you throw us into the fiery furnace, our God is able to save us. But even if he does not save us, you can be sure, O king, that we would not serve your gods or worship the golden statue you have erected." Upon hearing this, Nebuchadnezzar was filled with anger, and his face was distorted with rage against Shadrach, Meshach, and Abednego. He ordered his men to heat the fiery furnace seven times hotter than it usually was. He also commanded some of his mighty men to bind Shadrach, Meshach, and Abednego and throw them into the white-hot furnace. Immediately, they tied up the three men while they still had on all their clothes—their trousers, shirts, and turbans—and then threw them into the white-hot furnace. But because the king's command was so urgent and the furnace so overheated, the raging flames burned up the men who carried Shadrach, Meshach, and Abednego into the fire. And the three men, Shadrach, Meshach, and Abednego, tied and bound, fell inside the blazing, white-hot furnace. Suddenly King Nebuchadnezzar jumped up in amazement and asked his officials, "Didn't we throw three men, bound in fetters, into the fire?" "That is correct, Your Majesty," they answered him. "But look," he shouted, "I see four men walking about freely in the fire. They're all unharmed! And the fourth man has the appearance of a son of the gods!" Then Nebuchadnezzar cautiously approached the opening of the white-hot blazing furnace and shouted, "Shadrach, Meshach, and Abednego, servants of the Great God, come out here now!" So out of the midst of the fire walked Shadrach, Meshach, and Abednego completely unharmed. When all the kings' officials had assembled, along with the princes, magistrates, and governors, they discovered that the fire had not harmed these three men. Their hair was not singed, their clothes were not scorched, and they didn't even smell like smoke. King Nebuchadnezzar said, "Praise be to the God of Shadrach, Meshach, and Abednego! For he sent his divine messenger to rescue his servants who trusted in him. They disobeyed my orders and laid their lives on the line rather than serve or worship any god but their own. So I hereby make this decree: Any person from any nation or language who says anything against the God of Shadrach, Meshach, and Abednego will be torn limb from limb, and his house will be destroyed, because there is no other god who is able to rescue so miraculously!" Then the king promoted Shadrach, Meshach, and Abednego in the province of Babylon." Daniel 3 TPT

Think

How bold! How confident in God! I love that about these three men! And how sincere was their love for God? Even if He chose not to save them, they were at peace with dying and going to be with Him. They didn't demand anything from God or announce that He would do things their way. They were open to God being God and handling the situation however He chose.

They were thrown into the fire fully clothed and tied up. They didn't even smell like smoke after the fiery ordeal. God honored their faith so amazingly. They brought so much glory to God by staying strong and refusing to compromise. Their submission to God also allowed so many people to get a glimpse of the one true living God!

These are the same men who, with Daniel, didn't defile themselves with the king's impure food. Perhaps seeing God move in that situation helped build this unshakable faith and willingness to obey God. How important it is to keep remembering God's goodness and faithfulness that we've already seen in our lives!

Reflect

1. Who in your life tends to significantly influence your faith positively? Negatively?

2. Is there a specific circumstance that you're having a hard time surrendering to God and trusting Him to work out for His glory?

3. Think about a time when you've stood firm in your faith in the face of trials.

Pray

God, please help us to be so firmly rooted in You, that we aren't moved by circumstances or fear or anything else. You are more powerful than any of it. Give us peace when things don't go how we expect or desire. Thank You that You're always in control and always trustworthy, regardless of any experience we have. Help us to live in a way that shows we know how big You are. All the time, not just when we're comfortable and things are going our way. Help us to remember You've always been with us in every fire we've gone through and You won't stop. Help us not to make excuses for any disobedience and remember that You require full obedience. Thank You for loving us always.

TESTIFY

And Jethro rejoiced over all the goodness which the Lord had done for Israel, in rescuing them from the hand of the Egyptians.
Exodus 18:9 NASB

Jethro was delighted to hear about all the good things the Lord had done for Israel in rescuing them from the hand of the Egyptians.
Exodus 18:9 NIV

Read

Exodus 18:1-12.

"Now Jethro, the priest of Midian, Moses' father-in-law, heard about everything that God had done for Moses and for Israel His people, how the Lord had brought Israel out of Egypt. And Jethro, Moses' father-in-law, took in Moses' wife Zipporah, after he had sent her away, and her two sons, one of whom was named Gershom, for Moses said, "I have been a stranger in a foreign land." And the other was named Eliezer, for he said, "The God of my father was my help, and saved me from the sword of Pharaoh." Then Jethro, Moses' father-in-law, came with his sons and his wife to Moses in the wilderness where he was camped, at the mountain of God. And he sent word to Moses: "I, your father-in-law Jethro, am coming to you with your wife and her two sons with her." Then Moses went out to meet his father-in-law, and he bowed down and kissed him; and they asked each other about their welfare, and went into the tent. Moses told his father-in-law everything that the Lord had done to Pharaoh and to the Egyptians for Israel's sake, all the hardship that had confronted them on the journey, and how the Lord had rescued them. And Jethro rejoiced over all the goodness which the Lord had done for Israel, in rescuing them from the hand of the Egyptians. So Jethro said, "Blessed be the Lord who rescued you from the hand of the Egyptians and from the hand of Pharaoh, and who rescued the people from under the hand of the Egyptians. Now I know that the Lord is greater than all the gods; indeed, it was proven when they acted insolently against the people." Then Jethro, Moses' father-in-law, took a burnt offering and sacrifices for God, and Aaron came with all the elders of Israel to eat a meal with Moses' father-in-law before God." Exodus 18:1-12 NASB

Think

Word spread of everything God did for Moses and the Israelites. Jethro came to hear it for himself directly from Moses. It brought Jethro joy and delight and led him to worship God himself. He was able to enter the Presence of God with Moses, Aaron, and the other leaders of Israel.

As I read these verses, I think about what word I want to spread about my life. I want people to think about God's goodness when they think about my life. I want my experiences to point to God's glory. Moses had trials and hardships, but that wasn't his focus. His focus was on what God did. How God showed up and rescued Moses and all of the Israelites. How He saved them and helped them. How He did the "impossible."

I haven't personally seen a sea split in two or followed a moving fire through the wilderness to escape slavery. But God has certainly moved time and time again in my life. Sometimes in seemingly small, subtle ways and sometimes in more obvious ways. I know the same is true for you. We draw closer to God, grow our own faith, and give a boost to others' faith when we share those parts of our stories. And God loves to have us thinking about Him and being grateful for what He's done. It postures our hearts to receive a deeper revelation of who God is, to feel His love rather than fear of anything we are facing.

Reflect

1. Word traveled about what God did for Moses. When word travels about you, is it about overcoming hardships through God? Or is it more likely to be gossip or other negative things?

2. What have you personally seen God do for you? What are you grateful for right now? Have a thing or two ready to share in conversations to give hope and encouragement or even just to shift the conversation to a more positive path.

3. Be watchful in your communication and your thoughts for negativity, gossip, or anything else not pleasing to God. As soon as you identify any of these, replace it with positivity, kindness, and things pleasing to God. Read Philippians 4:8 and Colossians 3:1-8.

Pray

God, thank You for being with us always - in the hardships and troubles and when everything is going smoothly. Please help us to become more aware of You and stay focused on You. Help us to share with others because we love You so much we can't hold it in. Use the ways you've blessed us to bless the people we encounter. Let us bring others into Your Presence with us because there is nowhere better.

WISDOM

You will surely wear out, both yourself and these people who are with you,
because the task is too heavy for you; you cannot do it alone.
Exodus 18:18 NASB

You will certainly wear out both yourself and these people who are with you,
because the task is too heavy for you [to bear];you cannot do it alone.
Exodus 18:18 AMP

You and these people who come to you will only wear yourselves out. The work
is too heavy for you; you cannot handle it alone.
Exodus 18:18 NIV

And I spoke to you at that time, saying, 'I am not able to endure you alone.'
Deuteronomy 1:9 NASB

I spoke to you at that time, saying, 'I am not able to bear the burden of you
alone.'
Deuteronomy 1:9 AMP

At that time I said to you, "You are too heavy a burden for me to carry alone."
Deuteronomy 1:9 NIV

Read

Exodus 18:13-26 and Deuteronomy 1:9-17.

"And it came about the next day, that Moses sat to judge the people, and the people stood before Moses from the morning until the evening. Now when Moses' father-in-law saw all that he was doing for the people, he said, "What is this thing that you are doing for the people? Why do you alone sit as judge and all the people stand before you from morning until evening?" Moses said to his father-in-law, "Because the people come to me to inquire of God. When they have a dispute, it comes to me, and I judge between someone and his neighbor and make known the statutes of God and His laws." Moses' father-in-law then said to him, "The thing that you are doing is not good. You will surely wear out, both yourself and these people who are with you, because the task is too heavy for you; you cannot do it alone. Now listen to me: I will give you counsel, and God be with you. You be the people's representative before God, and you bring the disputes to God, then admonish them about the statutes and the laws, and make known to them the way in which they are to walk and the work they are to do. Furthermore, you shall select out of all the people able men who fear God, men of truth, those who hate dishonest gain; and you shall place these over them as leaders of thousands, of hundreds, of fifties, and of tens. Let them judge the people at all times; and let it be that they will bring to you every major matter, but they will judge every minor matter themselves. So it will be easier for you, and they will carry the burden with you. If you do this thing and God so commands you, then you will be able to endure, and all these people also will go to their places in peace." So Moses listened to his father-in-law and did everything that he had said. Moses chose able men out of all Israel and made them heads over the people, leaders of thousands, of hundreds, of fifties, and of tens. Then they judged the people at all times; they would bring the difficult matter to Moses, but they would judge every minor matter themselves." Exodus 18:13-26 NASB

"And I spoke to you at that time, saying, 'I am not able to endure you alone. The Lord your God has multiplied you, and behold, you are this day like the stars of heaven in number. May the Lord, the God of your fathers increase you a thousand times more than you are, and bless you, just as He has promised you! How can I alone endure the burden and weight of you and your strife? Obtain for yourselves men who are wise, discerning, and informed from your tribes, and I will appoint them as your heads.' And you answered me and said, 'The thing which you have said to do is good.' So I took the heads of your tribes, wise and informed men, and appointed them as heads over you, commanders of thousands, hundreds, fifties, and tens, and officers for your tribes. "Then I ordered your judges at that time, saying, 'Hear the cases between your fellow countrymen and judge righteously between a person and his fellow countryman, or the stranger who is with him. You are not to show partiality in judgment; you shall hear the small and the great alike. You are not to be afraid of any person, for the judgment is God's. The case that is too difficult for you, you shall bring to me, and I will hear it.'" Deuteronomy 1:9-17 NASB

Think

Literally, one man dealing with every argument and tough decision for hundreds of thousands of people? Let's think about that when we're having a bad day at work. Or think about being one of those hundreds of thousands of people going to get in line to wait for that one man! I've been known to decide I don't really need what I went shopping for if there are more than two people in line to make purchases. I digress - this reading isn't about patience (but feel free to pray for me if the Holy Spirit nudges you in that direction...). So, Moses. Surrounded by crowds. All. Day. Long. And not happy crowds waiting for a concert or sporting event. Crowds of people majorly stressed out because they had a dispute with a neighbor or friend. They feel wounded, misunderstood, scared, angry, etc. They don't know how to work it out or what God wants them to do. And I would imagine standing around waiting would intensify the disagreement and even lend itself to comparing the significance of the various disputes. "Seriously, I'm here with this huge issue and I have to wait behind these guys with such a silly little argument?!"

Jethro sees one day of this and realizes Moses cannot sustain this set up for long. It's not good for the people either (verse 18). Jethro gives Moses wisdom about leadership and delegation. He also tells Moses only to take his advice if God approves - beautiful humility and true wisdom for all of us. Sometimes we get great advice from friends and family. God blesses us through relationships. But we need to be careful to go to God for wisdom and to make sure those recommendations are approved by God. We also have to remember to take our struggles to God, not just other people, for help. James 1:5 tells us God gives wisdom generously to us when we ask for it.

Reflect

1. Is there something overwhelming you that you're trying to do/carry alone?

2. Do you ask God for wisdom throughout your day?

3. Do you tend to go to God first or other people first when you aren't sure what to do or feel overwhelmed? Do you have a reminder in place for yourself to go to God first?

Pray

God, thank You that we aren't meant to carry heavy burdens alone. You carry them with us and bring other people alongside us. Please bless us with heathy relationships and the help we need. We ask for Your wisdom. Thank You that You've already promised in Your Word to answer that request. Thank You that You care for us.

ETERNAL MINDSET

For this is the will of My Father, that everyone who sees the Son and believes in Him will have eternal life, and I Myself will raise him up on the last day.
John 6:40 NASB

For the longing of my Father is that everyone who embraces the Son and believes in him will experience eternal life and I will raise them up in the last day!
John 6:40 TPT

Read

John 6:25-40.

"When they finally found him, they asked him, "Teacher, how did you get here?" Jesus replied, "Let me make this very clear, you came looking for me because I fed you by a miracle, not because you believe in me. Why would you strive for food that is perishable and not be passionate to seek the food of eternal life, which never spoils? I, the Son of Man, am ready to give you what matters most, for God the Father has destined me for this purpose." They replied, "So what should we do if we want to do God's work?" Jesus answered, "The work you can do for God starts with believing in the One he has sent." They replied, "Show us a miracle so we can see it, and then we'll believe in you. Moses took care of our ancestors who were fed by the miracle of manna every day in the desert, just like the Scripture says, 'He fed them with bread from heaven.' What sign will you perform for us?" "The truth is," Jesus said, "Moses didn't give you the bread of heaven. It's my Father who offers bread that comes as a dramatic sign from heaven. The bread of God is the One who came out of heaven to give his life to feed the world." "Then please, sir, give us this bread every day," they replied. Jesus said to them, "I am the Bread of Life. Come every day to me and you will never be hungry. Believe in me and you will never be thirsty. Yet I've told you that even though you've seen me, you still don't believe in me. But everyone my Father has given to me, they will come. And all who come to me, I will embrace and will never turn them away. And I have come out of heaven not for my own desires, but for the satisfaction of my Father who sent me. My Father who sent me has determined that I will not lose even one of those he has given to me, and I will raise them up in the last day.

For the longing of my Father is that everyone who embraces the Son and believes in him will experience eternal life and I will raise them up in the last day!"" John 6:25-40 TPT

Think

Jesus had just fed the massive crowd with 5 bread rolls, 2 small fish, and a "thank You" to God. The crowd was filled and thrilled. Who doesn't love a free lunch? Jesus points out that He had been feeding them spiritually - by teaching them about God's Kingdom (Luke 9:11) and healing the sick. But they were searching for Him the next day because they wanted more free food, not because they wanted to follow Him or even because of the miracles He had done. Their priorities were all out of whack! Before we judge them too harshly, let's stop and examine our own hearts. If we're being honest, we've all had a time or two of seeking blessings rather than the One who gives them.

Jesus tells them (and us) to get an eternal mindset, rather than a worldly one. They seem to miss the point and ask Him what they can do to get in good with God and be able to generate more free food. Then they ask Jesus for a sign. Seriously?! He just spent the day before healing all the sick who were brought to Him AND giving them miraculous food from thin air. They still need "a sign!?" He corrects them yet again and tells them the key is to believe in Him. Stop focusing on the wrong thing. Jesus is the way to ETERNAL LIFE and they are missing it because they are distracted by the free meal. They (we) have to do the Father's will just like Jesus did while He walked this earth. God wants everyone to follow Him and live eternally.

Reflect

1. What miracles have you seen God do in your own life? How does this affect your relationship with Him?

2. Are there times when you lose sight of the big picture, getting caught up in circumstances whether good or bad?

3. Does your life show proof that You are following and obeying God?

Pray

God, please help us to focus on You first and foremost. Help us not to lose sight of You and Your love whether we're in the midst of a crisis or enjoying what You've blessed us with. Thank You for Your unfailing love.

Spiritual Nourishment

I am the living bread that came down out of heaven; if anyone eats from this bread, he will live forever; and the bread which I will give for the life of the world also is My flesh.
John 6:51 NASB

I alone am this living Bread that has come to you from heaven. Eat this Bread and you will live forever. The living Bread I give you is my body, which I will offer as a sacrifice so that all may live.
John 6:51 TPT

Read

John 6:41-59.

"When the Jews who were hostile to Jesus heard him say, "I am the Bread that came down from heaven," they immediately began to complain, "How can he say these things about himself? We know him, and we know his parents. How dare he say, 'I have come down from heaven?'" Jesus responded, "Stop your grumbling! The only way people come to me is by the Father who sent me—he pulls on their hearts to embrace me. And those who are drawn to me, I will certainly raise them up in the last day." Jesus continued, "It has been written by the prophets, 'They will all be taught by God himself.' If you are really listening to the Father and learning directly from him, you will come to me. For I am the only One who has come from the Father's side, and I have seen the Father! I speak to you living truth: Unite your heart to me and believe—and you will experience eternal life! I am the true Bread of Life. Your ancestors ate manna in the desert and died. But standing here before you is the true Bread that comes out of heaven, and when you eat this Bread you will never die. I alone am this living Bread that has come to you from heaven. Eat this Bread and you will live forever. The living Bread I give you is my body, which I will offer as a sacrifice so that all may live." These words of Jesus sparked an angry outburst among the Jews. They protested, saying, "Does this man expect us to eat his body?" Jesus replied to them, "Listen to this eternal truth: Unless you eat the body of the Son of Man and drink his blood, you will not have eternal life. Eternal life comes to the one who eats my body and drinks my blood, and I will raise him up in the last day. For my body is real food for your spirit and my blood is real drink. The one who eats my body and drinks my blood lives in me and I live in him. The Father of life sent me, and he is my life. In the same way, the one who feeds upon me, I will become his life. I am not like the bread your ancestors ate and later died. I am the living Bread that comes from heaven. Eat this Bread and you will live forever!" Jesus preached this sermon in the synagogue in Capernaum." John 41-59 TPT

Think

Ok, these verses make me cringe a little at first reading. The crowd is turning on Jesus because He's denied their request for more free food. And then Jesus's response seems a little out there. When we dig in (sorry - pun intended), we can see that Jesus is explaining that just as bread is food for the body; Jesus is food for the spirit. The "eating" is internalizing - taking Jesus into our beings, not a weird meal. The leaders didn't understand what Jesus was saying and mocked Him to the crowd. Unfortunately, this still happens a lot today. If you have any doubt, spend five minutes on social media.

Now that we have that cleared up, let's jump back up to Verse 41. They are grumbling about Jesus being the bread of heaven, which is reminiscent of the Israelites grumbling in the wilderness (see Exodus 16 and 17). Jesus proceeds to remind them about the bread God gave in the wilderness, and tell them how much more powerful, sustaining, and life-giving He is. He asserts that His power and authority are above that of Moses, and that believing that He has seen the Father and come from Him gives eternal life. Jesus offers them everything, but their hearts are hard and they can't understand.

Reflect

1. Do your blessings sometimes distract you from the One who gives those blessings?

2. What do you think internalizing Jesus looks like? How do you put that into practice?

3. Stop and think about having ETERNAL LIFE with Jesus - being with God and without tears or fears! Forever! How does shifting to an eternal perspective change how you view your life today?

4. Have you ever had your words twisted? Jesus knows exactly how that feels and He cares (see 2 Corinthians 1:3-4 and 1 Peter 5:7). If you haven't already done so, challenge yourself to forgive. And if you've been the one guilty of doing the twisting, seek forgiveness. He's faithful and He doesn't hold grudges.

Pray

Jesus, thank You for subjecting Yourself to mocking crowds and everything else You experienced, because of Your great love for us and Your obedience to the Father. Please give us soft hearts to understand, believe, and receive.

LOVE & LOYALTY

(Now Jesus loved Martha and her sister, and Lazarus.) So when He heard that he was sick, He then stayed two days longer in the place where He was.
John 11:5-6 NASB

Now even though Jesus loved Mary, Martha, and Lazarus, he remained where he was for two more days.
John 11:5-6 TPT

Read

John 11:1-16.

"In the village of Bethany there was a man named Lazarus, and his sisters, Mary and Martha. Mary was the one who would anoint Jesus' feet with costly perfume and dry his feet with her long hair. One day Lazarus became very sick to the point of death. So his sisters sent a message to Jesus, "Lord, our brother Lazarus, the one you love, is very sick. Please come!" When he heard this, he said, "This sickness will not end in death for Lazarus, but will bring glory and praise to God. This will reveal the greatness of the Son of God by what takes place." Now even though Jesus loved Mary, Martha, and Lazarus, he remained where he was for two more days. Finally, on the third day, he said to his disciples, "Come. It's time to go to Bethany." "But Teacher," they said to him, "do you really want to go back there? It was just a short time ago the people of Judea were going to stone you!" Jesus replied, "Are there not twelve hours of daylight in every day? You can go through a day without the fear of stumbling when you walk in the One who gives light to the world. But you will stumble when the light is not in you, for you'll be walking in the dark." Then Jesus added, "Lazarus, our friend, has just fallen asleep. It's time that I go and awaken him." When they heard this, the disciples replied, "Lord, if he has just fallen asleep, then he'll get better." Jesus was speaking about Lazarus' death, but the disciples presumed he was talking about natural sleep. Then Jesus made it plain to them, "Lazarus is dead. And for your sake, I'm glad I wasn't there, because now you have another opportunity to see who I am so that you will learn to trust in me. Come, let's go and see him." So Thomas, nicknamed the

Twin, remarked to the other disciples, "Let's go so that we can die with him."" John 11:1-16 TPT

Think

There are so many beautiful things in these passages that set the stage for something huge Jesus is going to do. These siblings have such a strong relationship with Jesus. They love Him and He loves them. Throughout the book of John, the author refers to himself as the disciple "whom Jesus loved." In Verse 3, Lazarus is identified as "the one You love." Verse 5 tells that Jesus loves all three of the siblings. The emphasis on love here is a great reminder that God is love (see 1 John 4:16). Jesus is love. Everything Jesus did, including waiting two more days before beginning His journey back to Lazarus, He did in love. Jesus waited until the right time even though He knew His friends were scared and hurting and calling out to Him for help.

Jesus decided to go back to Judea even though some of the leaders there had already attempted to kill Him and definitely still wanted Him dead. The disciples question this decision. Thomas gets a bad rap for needing evidence, but here he fully expects that Jesus is going to die at the hands of the leaders. He also thinks he and all the disciples will be murdered if they go with Him. Yet, he still is willing to go - talk about devotion!

Jesus was safe even going back to Judea because the time for Him to die hadn't come quite yet. He was in His Father's will so He was walking in the "daylight."

Reflect

1.   You are also the one Jesus loves. Fill in the blank with your name and say this out loud: "I am _____, the one Jesus loves." How does that feel?

2.   "I just love waiting! I always feel God's love when I'm waiting" said no one ever. Unless you have. If you have, please write to me and teach me your ways! But in general, waiting is hard and can feel lonely. Sometimes we feel like God isn't answering while we wait.

- Have you experienced this?

- Have you seen afterward what God was doing?

- Has it helped you grow and/or avoid heartache?

- Do you trust God's timing and plans for your life?

3.   Jesus was willing to walk right into the place where people plotted to kill Him. He knew His time hadn't come yet and how this would all play out. But His disciples didn't. Thomas really thought they'd all be murdered. And yet, he said, "Let's go." That kind of loyalty showed Jesus was really first in his life. Think of a time when you've boldly done something in faith that demonstrated putting God first. Did it go the way you thought it would? Did it end up giving you even more faith?

Pray

God, thank You that You are faithful and trustworthy. You work things together for our good, even when it doesn't seem apparent in the moment. You are love and You hear us when we call to You. Thank You for caring for us and about us. Every single one of us, right down to the smallest details.

FAITH

Jesus wept.
John 11:35 NASB

Then tears streamed down Jesus' face.
John 11:35 TPT

Read

John 11:17-37.

"Now when they arrived at Bethany, which was only about two miles from Jerusalem, Jesus found that Lazarus had already been in the tomb for four days. Many friends of Mary and Martha had come from the region to console them over the loss of their brother. And when Martha heard that Jesus was approaching the village, she went out to meet him, but Mary stayed in the house. Martha said to Jesus, "My Lord, if only you had come sooner, my brother wouldn't have died. But I know that if you were to ask God for anything, he would do it for you." Jesus told her, "Your brother will rise and live." She replied, "Yes, I know he will rise with everyone else on resurrection day." "Martha," Jesus said, "You don't have to wait until then. I am the Resurrection, and I am Life Eternal. Anyone who clings to me in faith, even though he dies, will live forever. And the one who lives by believing in me will never die. Do you believe this?" Then Martha replied, "Yes, Lord, I do! I've always believed that you are the Anointed One, the Son of God who has come into the world for us!" Then she left and hurried off to her sister, Mary, and called her aside from all the mourners and whispered to her, "The Master is here and he's asking for you." So when Mary heard this, she quickly went off to find him, for Jesus was lingering outside the village at the same spot where Martha met him. Now when Mary's friends who were comforting her noticed how quickly she ran out of the house, they followed her, assuming she was going to the tomb of her brother to mourn. When Mary finally found Jesus outside the village, she fell at his feet in tears and said, "Lord, if only you had been here, my brother would not have died." When Jesus looked at Mary and saw her weeping at his feet, and all her friends who were with her grieving, he shuddered with emotion and was deeply moved with tenderness and compassion. He said to them, "Where did you bury him?" "Lord, come with us and we'll show you," they replied. Then tears streamed down Jesus' face. Seeing Jesus weep caused many of the mourners to say, "Look how much he loved Lazarus." Yet others said, "Isn't this the One who opens blind eyes? Why didn't he do something to keep Lazarus from dying?"" John 11:17-37 TPT

Think

Again in these verses, we still haven't arrived at the miracle, but they are jam-packed with goodness. These open with the news that Lazarus had already been dead and buried for four days when Jesus arrives. Jesus waited where He was for two days after receiving the message, but it was over four days until He arrived. What a long four days those must have been! There was a Jewish superstition that a soul stayed by the grave for three days. Jesus waiting beyond that period meant no one could deny that Lazarus was completely dead with no hope of waking. There would be no mistake that Lazarus was just asleep or passed out.

Isn't it interesting that word spread that Jesus was coming? Clearly the disciples weren't being paranoid about the danger of heading back that way. People were watching and talking about Jesus. Before He even arrived, Martha went to meet Him. This seems like the reverse of when Jesus was previously at their home and Martha stayed back, caught up in the work, while Mary went to Jesus.

Martha and Jesus's conversation reveals how great Martha's faith was. Not even the death of her sibling could shake her from the revelation that her good friend Jesus was the Messiah, the Son of God. She didn't stop trusting Him even though it looked like He had let her down. He hadn't shown up in time to stop the tragedy, even though He could have.

I like that Mary also didn't hesitate to go to Jesus in the midst of all her pain and disappointment. She immediately put herself in a humble, worshiping position. And Jesus cared so greatly about her feelings, He was moved. He had empathy. Her weeping made Him weep.

The people there acknowledged how powerful His miracles were. They had tremendous faith that Jesus could have healed Lazarus until the moment he died. But their faith stopped at the point where Lazarus's life stopped. Healing him after he had died was outside the realm of possibility for them. They hadn't seen it done and didn't even think of it. Jesus was about to open their eyes to something new about Himself and push their faith even further.

Reflect

1. Why do you think Martha went out while Mary stayed behind?

2. Some scholars believe Verse 35 was more of an indignant utterance. Do you believe Jesus is unhappy with things that hurt you?

3. Ask God to show you His perspective on something you're

struggling with - an area that you haven't seen Him move in before.

Pray

God, thank You that You are compassionate and You always show up. You are completely trustworthy even when we can't see how You will work things out. Help us to have peace knowing that You will. Increase our faith and use our lives to bring You glory.

FULLY HUMAN

So Jesus, again being deeply moved within, came to the tomb. Now it was a cave, and a stone was lying against it.
John 11:38 NASB

Then Jesus, with intense emotions, came to the tomb—a cave with a stone placed over its entrance.
John 11:38 TPT

Read

John 11:38-44.

"Then Jesus, with intense emotions, came to the tomb—a cave with a stone placed over its entrance. Jesus told them, "Roll away the stone." Then Martha said, "But Lord, it's been four days since he died—by now his body is already decomposing!" Jesus looked at her and said, "Didn't I tell you that if you will believe in me, you will see God unveil his power?" So they rolled away the heavy stone. Jesus gazed into heaven and said, "Father, thank you that you have heard my prayer, for you listen to every word I speak. Now, so that these who stand here with me will believe that you have sent me to the earth as your messenger, I will use the power you have given me." Then with a loud voice Jesus shouted with authority: "Lazarus! Come out of the tomb!" Then in front of everyone, Lazarus, who had died four days earlier, slowly hobbled out—he still had grave clothes tightly wrapped around his hands and feet and covering his face! Jesus said to them, "Unwrap him and let him loose."" John 11:38-44 TPT

Think

Here we see an astonishing miracle performed simply by the spoken word of Jesus. What God says always comes to pass (see Luke 1:37). By trusting Him and acting in faith (rolling the stone away), the people were able to participate in the miracle and see the glory of God. The miracle wasn't dependent on their faith, but their faith allowed them to partner with God.

I love that Jesus didn't hold out on this miracle as if having already seen someone be raised from the dead might somehow diminish His Resurrection. Do we hold out sometimes to make sure we're the first to do something or have something? Do we wait rather than help someone else bring glory to God?

Reflect

1. Jesus was deeply moved (v. 38) - fully human. He wasn't ashamed to be a human or just acting like a human. Does this challenge your thinking of Jesus?

2. Imagine standing there witnessing this (Jesus being moved and the miracle of Lazarus coming back to life). What emotions do you feel?

3. See verse 40. Do you believe you can experience God's glory here and now by believing? Why or why not?

Pray

Jesus, thank You for humbling Yourself to become fully human. Thank You for the ultimate example of trusting God and doing His will on earth. Help us to bring You glory. Please give us awareness of the areas where we hold a limited view of You. Help us to trust You to do things we haven't seen before. Raise our expectations of what You can and will do.

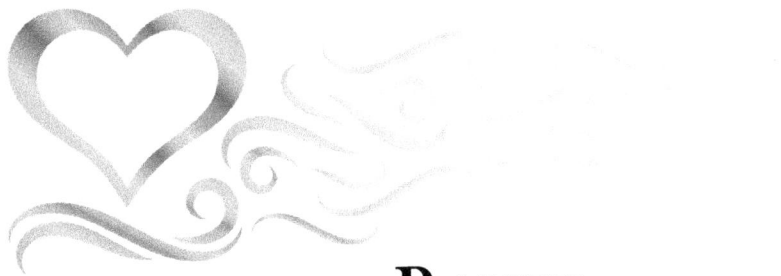

RAISED

And a poor man named Lazarus was laid at his gate, covered with sores,
Luke 16:20 NASB

Outside the gate of his mansion was a poor beggar named Lazarus.
Luke 16:20a TPT

Read

Luke 16:19-31.

"Jesus continued. "There once was a very rich man who had the finest things imaginable, living every day enjoying his life of opulent luxury. Outside the gate of his mansion was a poor beggar named Lazarus. He lay there every day, covered with boils, and all the neighborhood dogs would come and lick his open sores. The only food he had to eat was the garbage that the rich man threw away. One day poor Lazarus died, and the angels of God came and escorted his spirit into paradise. The day came that the rich man also died. In hell he looked up from his torment and saw Abraham in the distance, and Lazarus was standing beside him in the glory. The rich man shouted, 'Father Abraham! Father Abraham! Have mercy on me. Send Lazarus to dip his finger in water and come to cool my tongue, for I am in agony in these flames of fire!' But Abraham responded, 'My friend, don't you remember? While you were alive, you had all you desired. You surrounded yourself in luxury, while Lazarus had nothing. Now Lazarus dwells in the comforts of paradise and you are in agony. Besides, between us is a huge chasm that cannot be bridged, nor can anyone cross from one realm to the other, even if he wanted.' The rich man continued, 'Then let me ask you, Father Abraham, please send Lazarus to my relatives. Tell him to witness to my five brothers and warn them not to end up where I am in this place of torment.' Abraham replied, 'They've already had plenty of warning. They have the teachings of Moses and the revelation of the prophets; let them hear them.' 'What if they're not listening?' the rich man added. 'If someone from the dead were to go and warn them, they would surely repent.' Abraham said to him, 'If they wouldn't listen to Moses and the prophets, neither would they be convinced if someone were raised from the dead!'" Luke 16:19-31 TPT

Think

How I wish there was a description of Lazarus's four days in the tomb (see John 11:44)! However, I do find it quite interesting that this parable is the only one recorded with a name attached and also mention of someone being raised from the dead.

Perhaps Jesus was thinking of raising Lazarus while He was telling this parable. The timing is unclear because Jesus's miracle of raising Lazarus back to life is recorded in John and this parable is only recorded in Luke. If it was before He had done this amazing miracle, He would have been looking forward to it, knowing His plan. If it was after, hearing this parable would have brought to mind the greatest miracle the people had seen at that point.

Reflect

1. Who can you assist that is struggling right now?

2. Who in your life are you trusting God to rescue from spiritual darkness? Ask God if there is any action to take. Don't give up hope.

Pray

God, thank You that You save and deliver. You desire that everyone believe in You and be rescued from sin and eternal death and raised to life in You. Please help us to serve faithfully doing Your will. Let us share Your love and goodness to others.

PREPARED

but only one thing is necessary; for Mary has chosen the good part, which shall not be taken away from her.
Luke 10:42 NASB

but few things are needed—or indeed only one. Mary has chosen what is better, and it will not be taken away from her.
Luke 10:42 NIV

Mary has discovered the one thing most important by choosing to sit at my feet. She is undistracted, and I won't take this privilege from her.
Luke 10:42 TPT

Read

Luke 10:38-42.

"As Jesus and the disciples continued on their journey, they came to a village where a woman welcomed Jesus into her home. Her name was Martha and she had a sister named Mary. Mary sat down attentively before the Master, absorbing every revelation he shared. But Martha became exasperated with finishing the numerous household chores in preparation for her guests, so she interrupted Jesus and said, "Lord, don't you think it's unfair that my sister left me to do all the work by myself? You should tell her to get up and help me." The Lord answered her, "Martha, my beloved Martha. Why are you upset and troubled, pulled away by all these many distractions? Mary has discovered the one thing most important by choosing to sit at my feet. She is undistracted, and I won't take this privilege from her."" Luke 10:38-42 TPT

Think

We need to be prepared to encounter Jesus so we don't miss out. Maybe Martha was worried about her hospitality being criticized or not measuring up to the high standards of their culture. Maybe she just really wanted everything to be perfect for Jesus. But Jesus is the only perfect. We don't need to measure up; we need to sit at His feet and soak Him up and make Him the Lord of our lives.

Reflect

1. What distractions or busyness are you allowing to stand in your way of truly having fellowship with God?

2. Is concern about others' opinions an obstacle for your relationship with God?

3. What can you do to be more prepared to encounter Him?

Pray

God, help us to walk through life prepared to drop everything to be with You. Let us be willing to serve You wholeheartedly even if it brings criticism of others or means not keeping up appearances. Thank You that You value us enough to have personal, direct relationships with each of us.

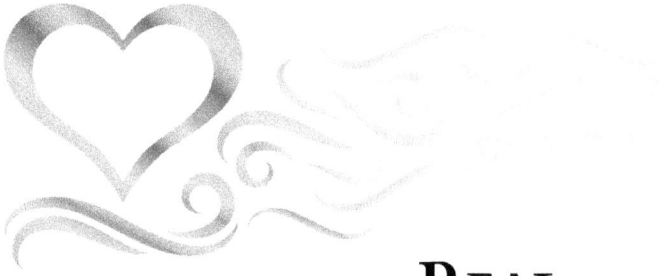

REAL

Nicodemus responded and said to Him, "How can these things be?"
John 3:9 NASB

Nicodemus said to Him, "How can these things be possible?"
John 3:9 AMP

Nicodemus replied, "I don't understand; what do you mean? How does this happen?"
John 3:9 TPT

Read

John 3:1-21.

"Now there was a prominent religious leader among the Jews named Nicodemus, who was part of the sect called the Pharisees. One night he discreetly came to Jesus and said, "Rabbi, we know that you are a teacher come from God, for no one performs the miracle signs that you do, unless God's power is with him." Jesus answered, "Nicodemus, listen to this eternal truth: Before a person can even perceive God's kingdom, they must first experience a rebirth." Nicodemus said, "Rebirth? How can a gray-headed man be reborn? It's impossible for anyone to go back into the womb a second time and be reborn!" Jesus answered, "I speak an eternal truth: Unless you are born of water and the Spirit, you will never enter God's kingdom. For the natural realm only gives birth to things that are natural, but the spiritual realm gives birth to supernatural life! You shouldn't be amazed by my statement, 'You all must be born from above!' For the Spirit-Wind blows as it chooses. You can hear its sound, but you don't know where it came from or where it's going. So it is the same with those who are Spirit-born!" Nicodemus replied, "I don't understand; what do you mean? How does this happen?" Jesus answered, "Nicodemus, aren't you the respected teacher in Israel, and yet you don't understand this revelation? I speak eternal truths about things I know, things I've seen and experienced—and still you don't accept what I reveal. If you're unable to believe what I've told you about the natural realm, what will you do when I begin to unveil the heavenly realm? No one has risen into the heavenly realm except the Son of Man who also exists in heaven. And just as Moses in the desert lifted up the brass replica of a venomous snake on a pole for all the people to see and be healed, so the Son of Man is ready to be lifted up, so that those who truly believe in him will not perish but be given eternal life. For here is the way God loved the world—he gave his only, unique Son as a gift. So now everyone who believes in him will never perish but experience everlasting life. God did not send his Son into the world to judge and condemn the world, but to be its Savior and rescue it! So now there is no longer any condemnation for those who believe in him, but the unbeliever already lives under condemnation because they do not believe in the name of the only Son of God. And here is the basis for their judgment: The Light of God has now come into the world, but the people loved darkness more than the Light, because they want the darkness to conceal their evil. So the wicked hate the Light and try to hide from it, for the Light fully exposes their lives. But those who love the truth will come into the Light, for the Light will reveal that it was God who produced their fruitful works." John 3:1-21 TPT

Think

Why did Nicodemus go to Jesus? He makes one statement and then Jesus makes a statement that changes the whole conversation. I love that Nicodemus was humble enough to ask what Jesus meant. At times, it can be tempting to just smile and nod and walk away with pride but no understanding. Nicodemus doesn't do that. He's comfortable admitting he doesn't know and as a result is able to gain important knowledge and wisdom (and in doing so, got it documented for all of us!).

I think it's really easy to judge all the Jews that had been awaiting the Messiah (their entire lives for generations) for missing Him. But human interpretations that gave inaccurate expectations were handed down right along with the prophecies. Jesus wasn't fitting the mold they had made for what the Messiah should come and do. How often do we miss what God is saying to us or that He is actually answering our prayers because it doesn't look like what we expect? We figure out how God should answer and assume he isn't answering when He does it His way instead of ours.

The bronze snake from Numbers 21 that Jesus references was a perfect example of not missing out because it doesn't make sense or seems completely weird. The Israelites were healed from deadly snake bites by just looking at the snake God had Moses make and hang up on a pole. What a way to learn to trust God! And what a beautiful example of obedience by Moses!

I love how Jesus clearly speaks of the flesh and spirit. The comparison to the wind is so vivid. We get eternal spiritual life because He loves us enough to give it to us. There is NO other way to take the gift given to us in love than by believing it's true. Thank You, God, for Your generous love lavished on us! Thank You for opening our hearts to allow us to believe.

Reflect

1. Think of a time when it seemed like God wasn't answering you until after the fact when you realized He was answering in a better way. What are some things you learned from that time?

2. Does being unable to logically comprehend specifically how God could work something out ever stand in the way of your faith? Read Proverbs 3:5 for a wonderful reminder.

Pray

God, please bring us new wisdom and clarity. Help us not to miss what You're doing because of how You're doing it. Help us to see our lives and other people from Your perspective. Thank You for Your unfailing love that moves our hearts.

LIGHT

This is the message we have heard from Him and announce to you, that God is Light, and in Him there is no darkness at all.
1 John 1:5 NASB

This is the life-giving message we heard him share and it's still ringing in our ears. We now repeat his words to you: God is pure light. You will never find even a trace of darkness in him.
1 John 1:5 TPT

Read

1 John 1:5-2:2.

"This is the life-giving message we heard him share and it's still ringing in our ears. We now repeat his words to you: God is pure light. You will never find even a trace of darkness in him. If we claim that we share life with him, but keep walking in the realm of darkness, we're fooling ourselves and not living the truth. But if we keep living in the pure light that surrounds him, we share unbroken fellowship with one another, and the blood of Jesus, his Son, continually cleanses us from all sin. If we boast that we have no sin, we're only fooling ourselves and are strangers to the truth. But if we freely admit our sins when his light uncovers them, he will be faithful to forgive us every time. God is just to forgive us our sins because of Christ, and he will continue to cleanse us from all unrighteousness. If we claim that we're not guilty of sin when God uncovers it with his light, we make him a liar and his word is not in us." I John 1:5-10 TPT

"You are my dear children, and I write these things to you so that you won't sin. But if anyone does sin, we continually have a forgiving Redeemer who is face-to-face with the Father: Jesus Christ, the Righteous One. He is the atoning sacrifice for our sins, and not only for ours but also for the sins of the whole world." I John 2:1-2 TPT

Think

Picture yourself in a gorgeous yard where you just finished planting flowers. The sun is shining, birds are chirping. Everything seems fresh and joyful. You're basking in the glory of God's creation, just feeling delighted to be alive, taking in deep satisfying breaths.

Then, out of the corner of your eye, a strange movement catches your attention. You stand and go to investigate. At the edge of the flowerbed, you find a surprise. Nope, sorry. Not a good surprise. The movement is a tangle of bugs. Not a handful of earthworms that will aerate the soil for your flowers. Nasty, ugly ones that make your stomach turn. Ones that make you feel like they're crawling on your skin.

Do you:

A. Quickly look around hoping your neighbors don't see this horrifying mess. Grab your welcome mat and relocate it hoping you'll block these critters' access to your yard.

B. Stand frozen to the spot screaming in terror.

C. Shrug your shoulders and say, "everything for a reason."

D. Call for help to find the source and fully rid your yard of these invaders.

Just like these bugs, sin is ugly and has to be dealt with. Jesus has complete victory over ALL sin. Dealing with it means examining yourself, recognizing it, and purging it. Examination is required because sin can be difficult to recognize. It's not always black and white, as simple as not stealing at the store or attacking someone who is irritating us to the extreme. Sin is also knowing what we should do but not doing it (see James 4:17).

Sin can creep in without us even realizing it in the moment. Left unchecked, it roots and grows. It creates a blockage in our hearts. Sin separates us from God's Presence. Sin weakens our spirits and our prayers. Sounds alarming, right? But here's the good news: Jesus conquered sin. We just have to bring our sin into the light and give it to Him. He forgives, we forgive ourselves, and we try to do better by drawing closer to Him. We don't need to grovel, beat ourselves up, or try to do extra good deeds. Just confess, accept the gift of forgiveness, and thank God for what He's done for us. What we could never accomplish for ourselves.

Reflect

1. Is it difficult for you to be vulnerable with God and confess your sin? Does it make it less intimidating to know that He already knows before you tell Him?

2. Do you believe God forgives you fully and immediately (see Colossians 2:14 and Isaiah 43:25)?

3. Are there different situations where you can relate to each of the answers A, B, C, and D above?

Pray

God, please help us to unabashedly step into Your light and come boldly before Your throne seeking grace and mercy. Thank You that You cleanse us fully and faithfully. You conquered all sin through Your incredible sacrifice.

LOVING CONFRONTATION

Jesus replied to her, "If you knew the gift of God, and who it is who is saying to you, 'Give Me a drink,' you would have asked Him, and He would have given you living water."
John 4:10 NASB

Jesus replied, "If you only knew who I am and the gift that God wants to give you, you'd ask me for a drink, and I would give you living water."
John 4:10 TPT

Read

John 4:1-30.

"The news quickly reached the Jewish religious leaders known as the Pharisees that Jesus was drawing greater crowds of followers coming to be baptized than John. (Although Jesus himself didn't baptize, but only his disciples.) Jesus heard what was being said and abruptly left Judea and returned to the province of Galilee, and he had to pass through Samaria. Jesus arrived at the Samaritan village of Sychar, near the field that Jacob had given to his son Joseph. Wearied by his long journey, he sat on the edge of Jacob's well, and sent his disciples into the village to buy food, for it was already afternoon. Soon a Samaritan woman came to draw water. Jesus said to her, "Give me a drink." She replied, "Why would a Jewish man ask a Samaritan woman for a drink of water?" (For Jews have no dealings with Samaritans.) Jesus replied, "If you only knew who I am and the gift that God wants to give you, you'd ask me for a drink, and I would give you living water." The woman replied, "But sir, you don't even have a bucket, and the well is very deep. So where do you find this 'living water'? Do you really think that you are greater than our ancestor Jacob who dug this well and drank from it himself, along with his children and livestock?" Jesus answered, "If you drink from Jacob's well, you'll be thirsty again, but if anyone drinks the living water I give them, they will never be thirsty again. For when you drink the water I give you, it becomes a gushing fountain of the Holy Spirit, flooding you with endless life!" The woman replied, "Let me drink that water so I'll never be thirsty again and won't have to come back here to draw water." Jesus said, "Go get your husband and bring him back here." "But I'm not married," the woman answered. "That's true,"

Jesus said, "for you've been married five times, and now you're living with a man who is not your husband. You have told the truth." The woman changed the subject. "You must be a prophet! So tell me this: Why do our fathers worship God on this nearby mountain, but your people teach that Jerusalem is the place where we must worship. Who is right?" Jesus responded, "Believe me, dear woman, the time has come when you will worship the Father neither on a mountain nor in Jerusalem, but in your heart. Your people don't really know the One they worship, but we Jews worship out of our experience, for it's from the Jews that salvation is available. From now on, worshiping the Father will not be a matter of the right place but with a right heart. For God is a Spirit, and he longs to have sincere worshipers who adore him in the realm of the Spirit and in truth." The woman said, "This is all so confusing, but I do know that the Anointed One is coming—the true Messiah. And when he comes, he will tell us everything we need to know." Jesus said to her, "You don't have to wait any longer, the Anointed One is here speaking with you—I am the One you're looking for." At that moment, his disciples returned and were stunned to see Jesus speaking with a Samaritan woman, yet none of them dared ask him why or what they were discussing. All at once, the woman left her water jar and ran off to her village and told everyone, "Come and meet a man at the well who told me everything I've ever done! He could be the One we've been waiting for." Hearing this, the people came streaming out of the village to go see Jesus." John 4:1-30 TPT

Think

I find it so interesting to think of Jesus being tired and thirsty. I forget about His human side sometimes. And I wonder how He felt to be among all these people who spent their whole lives watching for the Messiah but didn't recognize Him.

The term "living water" was used for a brook or creek as compared to the well water which was "still." The woman thinks Jesus is offering her an easier way to get water and she is all for it. Sometimes, we come to Jesus selfishly, too. What can You do for me? How can You make my life easier? The Bible clearly tells us that we'll have troubles and challenges (see John 16:33 and 1 Peter 4:12).

Jesus didn't tell her to bring her husband to shame her. It was customary at that time that a man wouldn't have a long (or any) conversation with a woman alone. So to keep the conversation going, He requested her husband join them. Of course, He knew her situation. Jesus was compassionate and loving but also confronted her sin. Because that is the loving thing to do. He was pointing it out and then rescuing her from it. He did it so gently that she didn't run away or stop taking to Him. I really wish I could hear their tones of voice in this conversation!

Reflect

1. What stands out to you as you read about Jews and Samaritans in the midst of today's racial tension and political unrest? Do you have pre-conceived notions about anyone currently that has

stopped you from getting to know them?

2. Is there anything in your life that Jesus is lovingly confronting? Ask Him to help you.

Pray

Holy Spirit, please make us aware of the areas we need to change and help us to depend on You to do it. Thank You that You faithfully lead and guide us. Help us to lovingly encourage others in the same way. Separating the sin from the sinner. Loving the sinner while hating the sin. Being a light, not a judge.

MARGIN

Keep watching and praying, so that you do not come into temptation; the spirit is willing, but the flesh is weak.
Matthew 26:41 NASB

Keep alert and pray that you'll be spared from this time of testing. Your spirit is eager enough, but your humanity is weak.
Matthew 26:41 TPT

Read

Matthew 26:36-46

"Then Jesus led his disciples to an orchard called "The Oil Press." He told them, "Sit here while I go and pray nearby." He took Peter, Jacob, and John with him. However, an intense feeling of great sorrow plunged his soul into agony. And he said to them, "My heart is overwhelmed and crushed with grief. It feels as though I'm dying. Stay here and keep watch with me." Then he walked a short distance away, and overcome with grief, he threw himself facedown on the ground and prayed, "My Father, if there is any way you can deliver me from this suffering, please take it from me. Yet what I want is not important, for I only desire to fulfill your plan for me." Then an angel from heaven appeared to strengthen him. Later, he came back to his three disciples and found them all sound asleep. He awakened Peter and said to him, "Could you not stay awake with me for even one hour? Keep alert and pray that you'll be spared from this time of testing. Your spirit is eager enough, but your humanity is weak." Then he left them for a second time to pray in solitude. He said to God, "My Father, if there is not a way that you can deliver me from this suffering, then your will must be done." He came back to the disciples and found them sound asleep, for they couldn't keep their eyes open. So he left them and went away to pray the same prayer for the third time. When he returned again to his disciples, he awoke them, saying, "Are you still sleeping? Don't you know the hour has come for the Son of Man to be handed over to the authority of sinful men? Get up and let's go, for the betrayer has arrived.""
Matthew 26:36-46 TPT

Think

I can relate to Peter, James, and John more than I'd like here. How often does God ask something simple of me and I don't do it? I get distracted or worn out and don't follow through. This is one of the reasons margin is so important. Having space for whatever He wants. Knowing that whatever my plans are might not be His and being ok with that. Being submitted exactly like Jesus in the garden.

If I truly believe God is all-knowing, why would I cling to my limited perspective of a situation, rather than trust Him?

Why did Jesus take them aside from the group but then put them in a different spot? Was it to give them a chance to partner in prayer with Him?

Was it because He wanted to teach them the importance of prayer and sometimes the hard way is the only way we learn? I think of Peter never denying Jesus again for the rest of his life (even during a gruesome death) after that rooster crowed.

Was it to have a reminder for all of us even 2,000 years later that we all fall short but it doesn't disqualify us (see Romans 3:23-25)?

Reflect

1. Are you over-scheduled or do you build space in your day for opportunities that pop up?

2. Proverbs 8:34 tells us to listen for wisdom daily. Is that a habit that you've formed?

Pray

Father God, You've never asked anything of us that comes close to what You asked of Jesus. Help us to be attuned to You so we don't miss Your instructions. Help us to hear Your voice and feel Your nudges clearly. Thank You, Holy Spirit, that You dwell in us and guide us. Thank You that Your grace equips us for every good work You have planned for us to do. Thank You that we get to be part of Your plans, vessels of Your goodness in this world. Please help us to realize and feel what a privilege that is, even when You ask us to do things that seem inconvenient at inopportune moments.

PRAYING

So he set out and came to his father. But when he was still a long way off, his father saw him and felt compassion for him, and ran and embraced him and kissed him.
Luke 15:20 NASB

So the young son set off for home. From along distance away, his father saw him coming, dressed as a beggar, and great compassion swelled up in his heart for his son who was returning home. The father raced out to meet him, swept him up in his arms, hugged him dearly, and kissed him over and over with tender love.
Luke 15:20 TPT

Read

Luke 15:11-31

"Then Jesus said, "Once there was a father with two sons. The younger son came to his father and said, 'Father, don't you think it's time to give me my share of your estate?' So the father went ahead and distributed between the two sons their inheritance. Shortly afterward, the younger son packed up all his belongings and traveled off to see the world. He journeyed to a far-off land where he soon wasted all he was given in a binge of extravagant and reckless living. With everything spent and nothing left, he grew hungry, because there was a severe famine in that land. So he begged a farmer in that country to hire him. The farmer hired him and sent him out to feed the pigs. The son was so famished, he was willing even to eat the slop given to the pigs, because no one would feed him a thing. Humiliated, the son finally realized what he was doing, and he thought, 'There are many workers at my father's house who have all the food they want with plenty to spare. They lack nothing. Why am I here dying of hunger, feeding these pigs and eating their slop? I want to go back home to my father's house, and I'll say to him, "Father, I was wrong. I have sinned against you. I'll never again be worthy to be called your son. Please, Father, just treat me like one of your employees."' So the young son set off for home. From a long distance away, his father saw him coming, dressed as a beggar, and great compassion swelled up in his heart for his son who was returning home. The father raced out to meet him, swept him up in his arms, hugged him dearly, and kissed him over and over with tender love. "Then the son said, 'Father, I was wrong. I have sinned against you. I could never deserve to be called your son. Just let me be—' The father interrupted and said, 'Son, you're home now!' Turning to his servants, the father said, 'Quick, bring me the best robe, my very own robe, and I will place it on his shoulders. Bring the ring, the seal of sonship, and I will put it on his finger. And bring out the best shoes you can find for my son. Let's prepare a great feast and celebrate. For my beloved son was once dead, but now he's alive! Once he was lost, but now he is found!' And everyone celebrated with overflowing joy. Now, the older son was out working in the field when his brother returned, and as he approached the house, he heard the music of celebration and dancing. He called over one of the servants and asked, 'What's going on?' The servant replied, 'It's your younger brother. He's returned home and your father is throwing a party to celebrate his homecoming.' The older son became angry and refused to go in and celebrate. So his father came out and pleaded with him, 'Come and enjoy the feast with us!' The son said, 'Father, listen! How many years have I worked like a slave for you, performing every duty you've asked as a faithful son? And I've never once disobeyed you. But you've never thrown a party for me because of my faithfulness. Never once have you even given me a goat that I could feast on and celebrate with my friends as this son of yours is doing now. Look at him! He comes back after wasting your wealth on prostitutes and reckless living, and here you are throwing a great feast to celebrate—for him!' The father said, 'My son, you are always with me by my side. Everything I have is yours to enjoy. It's only right to rejoice and celebrate like this, because your brother was once dead and gone, but now he is alive and back with us again. He was lost, but now he is found!'" Luke 15:11-31 TPT

Think

The Father celebrates when a lost one comes home. He leaves the 99 (represented by the older brother in this story) and runs to meet the lost 1 that's returning. There is a great deal of rejoicing. The son left and returned of his own free will.

It makes me think, too, about how important it is to be praying for all the people who we might not want to pray for. Praying for persecutors and enemies. Praying for people justly in prison. We know God can change any heart and we should always be excited for salvation and transformation, especially when it looks hopeless. God specializes in those situations. We have to be careful not to judge and to truly believe God can do anything.

The older brother who stayed with his father was bitter that his father hadn't given him even a young goat. But it sounds like he never asked for it. How often do we miss out on something God has for us simply because we don't ask? Prayer is so powerful and yet we can forget or not want to do it. God wants us to pray about everything, bringing Him into every area of our lives.

Reflect

1. Who do you identify with most in this story? Why?

2. Close your eyes and spend a few minutes envisioning God rejoicing over you personally. Absorb His love and desire to be known by you.

Pray

Thank You that we can always come back to You. Just like the prodigal son, we can just come back to You. Just like Jesus in the garden, we can just come back to You. You love our voices and the posture of our hearts when we are communicating with You. Thank You for hearing us and responding to us in the perfect ways. Give us a heart to seek You on behalf of others as well as ourselves.

GRACE & PEACE

Grace to you and peace from God our Father and the Lord Jesus Christ.
Philippians 1:2 NASB

May the blessings of divine grace and supernatural peace that flow from God our wonderful Father, and our Messiah, the Lord Jesus, be upon your lives.
Philippians 1:2 TPT

Read

Philippians 1:1-8.

"Paul and Timothy, servants of Christ Jesus, To all God's holy people in Christ Jesus at Philippi, together with the overseers and deacons: Grace and peace to you from God our Father and the Lord Jesus Christ. I thank my God every time I remember you. In all my prayers for all of you, I always pray with joy because of your partnership in the gospel from the first day until now, being confident of this, that he who began a good work in you will carry it on to completion until the day of Christ Jesus. It is right for me to feel this way about all of you, since I have you in my heart and, whether I am in chains or defending and confirming the gospel, all of you share in God's grace with me. God can testify how I long for all of you with the affection of Christ Jesus." Philippians 1:1-8 NIV

"From Paul and Timothy, both of us servants of Jesus, the Anointed One. To all his devoted followers in Philippi, including your pastors, and to all the servant-leaders of the church. May the blessings of divine grace and supernatural peace that flow from God our wonderful Father, and our Messiah, the Lord Jesus, be upon your lives. My prayers for you are full of praise to God as I give him thanks for you with great joy! I'm so grateful for our union and our enduring partnership that began the first time I presented to you the gospel. I pray with great faith for you, because I'm fully convinced that the One who began this gracious work in you will faithfully continue the process of maturing you until the unveiling of our Lord Jesus Christ! It's no wonder I pray with such confidence, since you have a permanent place in my heart! You have remained partners with me in the wonderful grace of God even though I'm here in chains for standing

up for the truth of the gospel. Only God knows how much I dearly love you with the tender affection of Jesus, the Anointed One."
Philippians 1:1-8 TPT

Think

Grace and peace are from God. Imitating Jesus requires extending grace to others and seeking to be at peace with others (see Romans 12:18). This isn't always easy, but God makes it possible when we align ourselves with Him. How do we do that? With thanksgiving and joyful prayer! Joy comes naturally when we spend time with God and keep our focus on Him, rather than our circumstances (see Psalm 121:2).

That being said, we are all works in progress. No one is complete in this life. Don't be hard on yourself for where you're at, but don't give up and stay there. Just keep going in the right direction - growing spiritually and knowing God better. Everyone has to keep learning and growing because God is infinite. No one can fully comprehend Him, but He does reveal Himself when we seek Him (see Jeremiah 29:12-13).

Because He loves us more than we can even comprehend, we can extend love to others. His undeserved forgiveness allows us to extend forgiveness to others and be peacemakers. He ransomed us so we can live for Him, joyfully and peacefully (see Colossians 3:15-17).

Reflect

1. It is a privilege to speak with the Creator of the universe. Do you pray with joy and confidence? Do you come to Him with thankfulness for what He's done even in the midst of undesirable circumstances?

2. We need to forgive ourselves and others in order to be at peace. Do you have someone that you need to forgive? What is one practical thing you could do to move in the right direction this week? See Romans 12:9-21 for some extra inspiration.

Pray

God, please help us to be holy as You are holy. Thank you that we are called out and set aside for You. We are Yours. Thank You that our lives are filled with Your grace and peace. You lavish it upon us in our undeserving state. You are a good, good Father. Thank You that we can come before You freely with our requests in prayer with joy. You listen to us faithfully and empower us through grace to spread the Gospel fearlessly. We will do this personally and by partnering with others. Thank You that when we accepted Jesus, You began a good work in us. Thank You that the Holy Spirit dwells in us and leads us and guides us to grow, mature, and become more like Christ. Thank You that You will continue to work on us daily – all the days of our lives. Thank You for never giving up on us! Thank You that we can enjoy Your peace and joy even when we fall short. We will still return to You and accept Your forgiveness. We will seek You wholeheartedly and find You and Your favor. No matter what circumstances we experience, we will know You are present and faithful. We will not be discouraged in our faith, Your promises, or any current situation. We will know that You love us unconditionally and fight to further Your Kingdom.

Unity & Discernment

And this I pray, that your love may overflow still more and more in real knowledge and all discernment,
Philippians 1:9 NASB

And this I pray, that your love may abound more and more [displaying itself in greater depth] in real knowledge and in practical insight,
Philippians 1:9 AMP

I continue to pray for your love to grow and increase beyond measure, bringing you into the rich revelation of spiritual insight in all things.
Philippians 1:9 TPT

Read

Philippians 1:9-11.

"I continue to pray for your love to grow and increase beyond measure, bringing you into the rich revelation of spiritual insight in all things. This will enable you to choose the most excellent way of all—becoming pure and without offense until the unveiling of Christ. And you will be filled completely with the fruits of righteousness that are found in Jesus, the Anointed One—bringing great praise and glory to God!"
Philippians 1:9-11 TPT

Think

It takes faith and God's power to love unconditionally because we all fall short (See Romans 3:23). Praying for others is one of the best ways to grow in love and receive God's grace to forgive them.

It's important to pray for the whole Body of Christ, not just the people we like and feel good about. Praying for everyone helps bring unity. Unity doesn't mean we agree about everything, but it does help us to value human beings because God loves every single one of us and we are ALL made in His image (see Romans 5:8 and Genesis 1:27).

When we pray, the Holy Spirit responds. Knowledge and wisdom come from Him and bring discernment, helping us to live better and do God's will. Prayer brings us deeper into relationship with God and improves other relationships when we allow Him to work on us.

Righteousness comes only from Jesus, not anything we can say or do. When we recognize that and really take it to heart, we become more teachable and usable for God's Kingdom. Dependence on Jesus grows compassion in us and allows us to see others through a lens of love.

Reflect

1. Do you pray for all believers? If all of your prayers were answered, would it change the world?

2. When we know someone intimately, we can have a sense of their thoughts and feelings, i.e. discern how they will likely think of or respond to something. When we spend time with God, we gain discernment to see things from His perspective. Is there something that you are struggling to see from a healthy perspective?

Pray

God, we ask to experience fresh revelations of You. To know You as a tender, loving, compassionate God. Please help us to extend that love to others and care for them and one another. Let us love selflessly and find joy in serving You.

We will grow in our knowledge of You and also our understanding. We will not just know about You; we will know You. We will live in communion with Your Holy Spirit and discern spirits. We will grasp what You've done for us and how much You care for us. We will know right from wrong, good from bad, and important from unnecessary. We will choose You and Your ways and wait expectantly for Your return. We will live with purity and humility, knowing that all that we are and all that we have comes from You.

Because we are set apart and have received the gift of salvation, our lives will display good character and righteousness that comes from our faith in You. We will bring glory and praise to You, God. We will keep You first in our lives. Thank You that we are part of Your bigger plan and that You will use us to further Your Kingdom. Please help us to keep a healthy, godly perspective even when things seem to be falling apart and we aren't where we want to be.

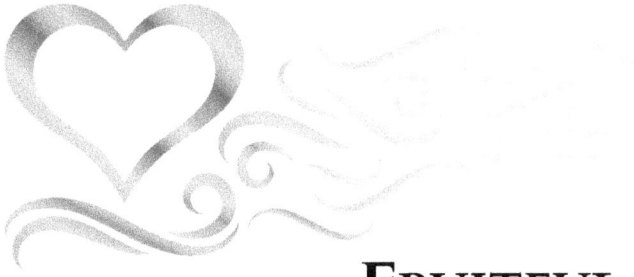

FRUITFUL

Now I want you to know, brothers and sisters, that my circumstances have turned out for the greater progress of the gospel,
Philippians 1:12 NASB

Now I want you to know, believers, that what has happened to me [this imprisonment that was meant to stop me] has actually served to advance [the spread of] the good news [regarding salvation].
Philippians 1:12 AMP

I want you to know, dear ones, what has happened to me has not hindered, but helped my ministry of preaching the gospel, causing it to expand and spread to many people.
Philippians 1:12 TPT

Read

Philippians 1:12-14.

"I want you to know, dear ones, what has happened to me has not hindered, but helped my ministry of preaching the gospel, causing it to expand and spread to many people. For now the elite Roman guards and government officials overseeing my imprisonment have plainly recognized that I am here because of my love for the Anointed One. And what I'm going through has actually caused many believers to become even more courageous in the Lord and to be bold and passionate to preach the Word of God, all because of my chains." Philippians 1:12-14 TPT

Think

Our job as followers of Christ is to further the Gospel, not just do good things. God planned good works for us to do (see Ephesians 2:10). We need to do *those* things, not as many random good deeds as we can think of. We are saved by God's grace, not by following a checklist of "shoulds" (see Galatians 2:16, Romans 11:6, and Ephesians 2:8-9).

Obeying God's will, regardless of what it looks like to others, is our assignment. It will look different for each of us and we can't compare our assignment to anyone else's (see Romans 12:4-5). It may seem insignificant, but the five loaves and two fish also seemed pretty insignificant until brought to Jesus and surrendered (see John 6:9)

Furthering the Gospel requires confidence and tenacity. It also requires joy. People are looking for joy, not burdensome rules or condemnation.

Laboring for God produces love, joy, peace, kindness. Being obedient to His calling will transform us, making our lives appealing to others.

Reflect

1. There is a difference between busyness and fruitfulness. Are there times when you value being busy over being obedient and fruitful?

2. Busyness can be a form of procrastination. If God wants me to write a book, but I crowd out my time with reading a book and volunteering in my neighborhood, I'm not being obedient, even though I'm being generous and seeking knowledge. We don't get a pass on disobedience just because we're doing something that appears righteous. Disobedience is sin even if it looks good to others. Is there something good in your life that you should be saying no to because it isn't really what God wants you to use your resources on right now?

3. We have to be intentional about being content with where God puts us and what He assigns so that others aren't turned off by our attitude or negativity (see Philippians 4:11-13). Staying positive can assist in drawing others to the Gospel. Are there times when you are unhappy with what God is asking you to do? How do you respond?

Pray

Please help us to remember that spreading the Gospel and being instruments of Your will and purpose are our goals and mission for this life. Help us to hear You clearly and follow Your prompting to serve You and reach people for You. Please help us to be relentless in our pursuit of You and outreach to others. We will not be discouraged or swayed or distracted from our calling. We will walk out our faith in boldness and obedience to You. Our actions will reflect our belief in and dependence on You. We will encourage others and see them saved, delivered, and on fire for You. We will know You well enough to represent You and fearlessly share You. Our motives will remain pure and we will not attempt to bring ourselves glory or personal gain.

JOY

What then? Only that in every way, whether in pretense or in truth, Christ is proclaimed, and in this I rejoice. But not only that, I also will rejoice,
Philippians 1:18 NASB

Yet in spite of all of this I am overjoyed! For what does it matter as long as Christ is being preached? If they preach him with mixed motives or with genuine love, the message of Christ is still being preached. And I will continue to rejoice
Philippians 1:18 TPT

Read

Philippians 1:15-30.

"It's true that there are some who preach Christ out of competition and controversy, for they are jealous over the way God has used me. Many others have purer motives—they preach with grace and love filling their hearts, because they know I've been destined for the purpose of defending the revelation of God. Those who preach Christ with ambition and competition are insincere—they just want to add to the hardships of my imprisonment. Yet in spite of all of this I am overjoyed! For what does it matter as long as Christ is being preached? If they preach him with mixed motives or with genuine love, the message of Christ is still being preached. And I will continue to rejoice because I know that the lavish supply of the Spirit of Jesus, the Anointed One, and your intercession for me will bring about my deliverance. No matter what, I will continue to hope and passionately cling to Christ, so that he will be openly revealed through me before everyone's eyes. So I will not be ashamed! In my life or in my death, Christ will be magnified in me. My true life is the Anointed One, and dying means gaining more of him. So here's my dilemma: Each day I live means bearing more fruit in my ministry; yet I fervently long to be liberated from this body and joined fully to Christ. That would suit me fine, but the greatest advantage to you would be that I remain alive. So you can see why I'm torn between the two—I don't know which I prefer. Yet deep in my heart I'm confident that I will be spared so I can add to your joy and further strengthen and mature your faith. When I am freed to come to you, my deliverance will give you a reason to boast even more in Jesus Christ. Whatever happens, keep living your lives based on the reality of the gospel of Christ. Then when I come to see you, or hear good reports of you, I'll know that you stand united in one Spirit and one passion—celebrating together as conquerors in the faith of the gospel. And then you will never be shaken or intimidated by the opposition that rises up against us. Your courage will prove to be a sure sign from God of their coming destruction. For God has graciously given you the privilege not only to believe in Christ, but also to suffer for him. For you have been called by him to endure the conflict in the same way I have endured it—for you know I'm not giving up." Philippians 1:15-30 TPT

Think

God can use anything for His glory. Seemingly horrible situations can further His Kingdom. Seek His perspective and remember that the Kingdom of Heaven doesn't operate on the same principles as the world's (see Romans 14:17-18).

It takes courage and hopeful expectation to live for God and do His will. It isn't always easy or neat. It gets messy, ugly, challenging. God's ways aren't our ways and trials can make us lose sight of the big picture. Praying helps combat that natural tendency and keep our faith and joy strong.

Live for Christ above all. Seek to honor Him in all situations. As a believer, our job is to faithfully share the Good News of God's redemptive work with others. God calls each of us to do this in different ways. Obeying His instructions in our own lives fits into His larger plan. Our efforts might seem smaller or less glamorous than someone else's, but that is not God's perspective (see Romans 12:3-8).

Reflect

1. We need to rejoice at God's Good News being advanced. Do you value the Kingdom of God more than the other things in your life? Do you celebrate the victories over darkness with the same vigor as physical, material blessings?

2. Prayers change things! Use your prayer time to come into agreement with God. Trust that He will make a way and work things out for true good, not just what might seem good in the moment.

Pray

We will gladly receive what You provide to us and believe that You are always more than enough. We will rejoice in all things and see Your goodness. Please help us to see things from Your perspective and live joyfully. We will not be taken captive by shame or guilt. We will live in the freedom, peace, and joy that can only be found in a solid relationship with You. Believing in and serving You will not be a chore; it will be the joyful fulfillment that our souls seek. Our eternal perspective will fuel us on to bold action for You and carry us when things seem dark and grim. We will trust You, remember You are Lord over all, and refuse to let troubles move us from the Rock.

ACKNOWLEDGEMENTS

The fact that you're holding this book right now is a testament to the skill of Dave at We Help Authors. Thanks, Dave, for your brilliant expertise and encouragement (and firm nudges when necessary)! And thank you, Stacy, for being the strongest support anyone could ask for.

A huge thank you to Cindy for formatting with peace, patience, and joy. Thank you for being such a loyal, loving sis!

Thank you to Early Risers (and thank you, Marcie, for the invite!) for helping me establish the habit of spending time with God bright and early everyday. So many of these devotions came during those quiet times with the Holy Spirit. Thank you for being so supportive as I began sharing!

And thank you to my sons for reading all of these before I was brave enough to share them with anyone else. I'm so proud of you for who you are (that could be another whole book so I'll stop myself). Thank you for all of your encouragement and patience. Love you so much!

ABOUT THE AUTHOR

Lori is the creator of the BB&B (Brain, Breath, & Breakthrough) trauma healing technique™ and a certified life breakthrough coach. She's passionate about loving God and helping others encounter Him. She loves seeing people get free of lies they've believed about themselves and God so they can flourish into who God created them to be. Lori is full of joy and empathy. Her sense of humor, openness about her own life, and sensitivity to the Holy Spirit create a space for healing and transformation. She's helped hundreds of people overcome the devastating effects of trauma and walk into new lives through individual sessions and her workshops. Lori lives in Chicago with her three sons.

CLARITY LIFE SOLUTIONS

Experiencing anxiety?

Feeling bad about yourself?

Experienced childhood trauma?

Frequently triggered?

Losing hope things will ever improve?

Ready for better?

BB&B Trauma Healing is for you! Rooted in cutting edge research and understanding of how the brain works, deeper healing is now available. Using highly effective trauma healing/clearing techniques, you can experience deep, lasting healing and remove triggers. Healing doesn't have to be a long, difficult process involving talking about the details of what you've been through. Lori can hold space for anything you want to share, but healing is just as effective without sharing anything at all.

Schedule a 90-minute Trauma Clearing Session with Lori and be amazed at how quickly years of old hurts and mountains of stress can be removed. **It's time for your breakthrough and transformation!**

ClarityLifeSolutions.com

WE HELP
AUTHORS

Want to write a book?

WeHelpAuthors.com specializes in
taking you from idea to published author.

Our team provides everything you need:
Book Planning & Strategy
Writing & Editing
Design & Formatting
Publishing & Marketing

Visit **WeHelpAuthors.com**
or email support@wehelpauthors.com
to start your author journey today.

www.ingramcontent.com/pod-product-compliance
Lightning Source LLC
Chambersburg PA
CBHW051821090426
42736CB00011B/1593